Books by Natalie Babbitt

AS AUTHOR

Tuck Everlasting (1975)
The Eyes of the Amaryllis (1977)
Herbert Rowbarge (1982)
The Moon Over High Street (2011)

AS AUTHOR AND ILLUSTRATOR

Dick Foote and the Shark (1967)
Phoebe's Revolt (1968)
The Search for Delicious (1969)
Kneeknock Rise (1970)
The Something (1970)
Goody Hall (1971)
The Devil's Storybook (1974)
The Devil's Other Storybook (1987)
Nellie: A Cat on Her Own (1989)
Bub: Or the Very Best Thing (1994)
Elsie Times Eight (2001)
Jack Plank Tells Tales (2007)

AS ILLUSTRATOR

The Forty-Ninth Magician by Samuel Babbitt (1966)
Small Poems by Valerie Worth (1972)
Still More Small Poems by Valerie Worth (1978)
Curlicues: The Fortunes of Two Pug Dogs by Valerie Worth (1980)
Small Poems Again by Valerie Worth (1986)
All the Small Poems and Fourteen More by Valerie Worth (1994)
Peacock and Other Poems by Valerie Worth (2002)

Barking with the Big Dogs

Natalie Babbitt

Barking with the Big Dogs

ON WRITING AND READING BOOKS FOR CHILDREN

Introduction by Katherine Applegate

FARRAR STRAUS GIROUX | NEW YORK

Farrar Straus Giroux Books for Young Readers
An imprint of Macmillan Publishing Group, LLC
175 Fifth Avenue, New York, NY 10010

First edition, 2018

1 3 5 7 9 10 8 6 4 2

fiercereads.com

Library of Congress Cataloging-in-Publication Data

Names: Babbitt, Natalie, author.
Title: Barking with the big dogs : on writing and reading books for children /
    Natalie Babbitt.
Description: First edition. | New York : Farrar Straus Giroux, [2018] | "A
    collection of essays and speeches by Natalie Babbitt"
Identifiers: LCCN 2018002807 | ISBN 9780374310400 (hardcover)
Subjects: LCSH: Children's literature, American—History and criticism. |
    Children—Books and reading.
Classification: LCC PS490 B43 2018 | DDC 810.9/9282—dc23
LC record available at https://lccn.loc.gov/2018002807

Our books may be purchased in bulk for promotional, educational, or business use.
Please contact your local bookseller or the Macmillan Corporate and Premium Sales
Department at (800) 221-7945, ext. 5442 or by email at
MacmillanSpecialMarkets@macmillan.com.

Frontispiece photograph of the author by Jesse Zellner

For my dear "Boss," Michael di Capua,
who published my first verse, then encouraged me to try prose,
and stuck with me for more than fifty years as muse and editor

Contents

Introduction

BY KATHERINE APPLEGATE

E very now and then, if the fates are kindly disposed, you will come across a book and know, as certainly as you know your own soul, that it was written just for you.

I have a few such cherished books on my office bookshelf. And one of them—a signed first edition, no less—just happens to be a picture book by the inimitable Natalie Zane Babbitt.

During her remarkable career, Natalie Babbitt gave us many opportunities to fall under the spell of her storytelling magic, including *Kneeknock Rise,* for which she was awarded a Newbery Honor, and her beloved modern classic, *Tuck Everlasting.*

But for me, it is one of her picture books—*Nellie: A Cat on Her Own*—that will always be first in my heart.

I was in my thirties when I came across the title, which by then had already been released in paperback. I'd been trying to educate myself about children's books, secretly wondering if I might be able to write one someday, secretly doubting I could ever pull it off.

In the book's charming cover illustration, Nellie, a wooden cat marionette, sits in a straw hat bedecked with pink ribbon, staring—contentedly, it would seem—into the distance. The interior art is equally beguiling. (A lifelong pet owner, Babbitt's drawings of dogs and cats practically bound off the page, their expressions every bit as nuanced as those of her humans.)

But while the art is gorgeous, it's the story that snared me. Nellie's life is tidily secure until the clever old woman who created her dies. How will the little toy survive, let alone dance, without someone's help? With the encouragement of a real cat named Big Tom, Nellie learns to face her fears and embrace her independence. By the end of the tale, we see her dancing joyfully in the moonlight, reveling in her "fine view of the wide, wild world."

It's a lovely fantasy, delicately told. But, as with all Natalie Babbitt's work, it's more, so much more, than that. In a mere handful of pages, this slender book challenges its readers to wrestle with big questions. How do we define independence? What does it mean to "belong to yourself"? How do we confront our darkest fears in order to claim the light as our own?

When I went on to read *Tuck Everlasting*, there they were again: big questions, this time the most ancient and profound of all. Why must we die? Would it be better to be immortal? How do we press on with our lives, knowing that eventually, as Winnie Foster says, "we all just go out, like the flame of a candle"?

To be honest, *Nellie* and *Tuck* left me vaguely melancholy for a while. It hurt a little to read them. They glittered too brightly with truth. And yet they were undeniably, at their hearts, resolutely hopeful stories.

When I read this fascinating collection of Babbitt's speeches and essays, it came as no surprise, then, that the importance of truth-telling in children's literature is a thematic touchstone. In all these pieces, Natalie Babbitt is unfailingly generous with her own truths as well; we learn a great deal about her fears, her loves, her work, her hopes. At the same time, we're also treated to an intriguing insider's view of children's literature as it evolved over four decades after she began publishing in 1966.

We read about an era when literature for teens (not yet dubbed "Young Adult") was still in its embryonic phase. We nod in resigned agreement as Babbitt grumbles about the advent of email. We applaud as she decries the way pleasurable childhood reading has given way to assigned drudge work.

And we laugh. A lot.

How I wish I'd had the pleasure of meeting Natalie Babbitt in person! The Michigander in me loves the no-nonsense, down-to-earth midwesterner's voice that animates her prose. (Although she moved dozens of times, her family roots were in Ohio.) Her humor is abundant, dry, and delightful. She is self-deprecating, especially about her vocation: "We're rather a motley crew, we makers of stories and pictures." (She's got *that* right.) And I loved this: "The world looks at us in a puzzled way and wonders, 'Why devote your life to writing for a group that has no money, no experience, and can't spell *rhinoceros*? Such writing can't be serious.'"

Babbitt can be tough on children's books, at least the sloppy, "Pepto-Bismol pink" variety, but only because she knows children deserve the absolute best literature we can give them. She adores teachers and librarians, the true and unsung heroes, she believes, of children's literature. But it is children themselves for whom she reserves her deepest love and respect. And because she respects her young readers, she knows their books can be hopeful without being condescending. Her stories, like all the best fantasies, are optimistic at their core. She doesn't "deny the dark." She "simply reaffirms the light."

"Facing the unfaceable," she calls it. Perhaps that's one of her greatest gifts to us: Natalie Babbitt is not afraid to write about being afraid. In fact, she concludes that *Nellie: A Cat on Her Own*— my beloved picture book—is at its essence a "mini-autobiography" about her own fears. (An epiphany that came with a nudge from her psychologist son.) Babbitt claims she was a somewhat timid child who grew into a risk-averse adult, a homebody at heart. She protests that she is not and never could be a true pathfinder, an intrepid Winnie, the kind of person who walks into the woods in search of adventure, or an adventurous Nellie, happily dancing alone while bathed in moonshine and magic.

But of course Natalie Babbitt *was* a pathfinder. She took huge and daring risks with her writing. Like Maurice Sendak and E. B. White, she led children toward the dark places where other writers were afraid to venture. And with every marvelous fantasy, every "good story, well told," she taught young readers how to name their fears, and thus become the heroes of their own stories.

"It wasn't my idea," Babbitt writes in her preface about creating this collection, but we are grateful indeed it exists. And while we enjoy her wise words, she's no doubt ensconced in the heavenly library she describes in one of her speeches, the place where "Lewis Carroll and J. M. Barrie and E. B. White and Beatrix Potter and Arnold Lobel and Arthur Rackham and Margot Zemach and all the others who have added so much to our lives meet every morning for milk and cookies and have a good time talking shop."

What excellent company she must be! For the rest of us, this brilliant book, with her fine view of the wide, wild world, is the next best thing.

Barking with the Big Dogs

Preface

There is in Rhode Island a woman who knows her way around an aphorism. She has created some wonders, from one of which the title for this collection of essays and speeches is taken. Her name is Julie Springwater, and the complete aphorism, which she gave me permission to adapt and use, says: "It came from barking with the big dogs." I have been drawn to, and bemused by, this one since I first saw it printed on a handsome little magnet. "The big dogs" has come at last to mean, for me professionally, the people who are out there in the adult field, writers who mostly have the real clout in the author-critic-analyst business. They are the ones in the forefront, the ones who seem to have the most to say (or bark), can say (or bark) it the loudest, and are saying (or barking) it most often.

Not that we in the children's field are silent when it comes to criticism and analysis. It's just that the noise we make in the literary world at large doesn't amount to much. Still, published writing is published writing regardless of its intended audience, so it's fair to point out that much of what needs saying, in regard to goings-on, can be said effectively from both fields.

However, effective is as effective does. Our noise, like that in the adult field, is made most memorably, and most objectively, not by our writers of fiction but by our well-trained, well-read teachers and editors, and if the truth be known, I feel that's where it should stay. Nevertheless, we makers of books are endlessly asked to produce speeches and articles, and after a while they begin to pile up. Collecting them this way, one puts oneself in the path of some rather unattractive assumptions on the part of readers about the weight of one's self-esteem. But it wasn't my idea. A bunch of people have said to me, over the years, "You should put all that stuff into a book." So I thought I might as well. At the very least, it gets it out of the file cabinet.

I don't do many speeches or articles these days. Enough is enough. But it's interesting, quite apart from who wrote them, to look back over the contents of any collection like this one where, if things are arranged chronologically, it's possible to see how the holding and defending of our opinions change, little by little, as we get older, and how what we choose to write about reflects what's going on in the world around us. Thirty-four years separate the first and the last entry in this volume, and nothing much has been altered except for a comma here and there, so it's easy to recognize the effect of the passing of time. How firmly we bark while we're young! And this in spite of the fact that we aren't nearly as comfortable with ourselves as we will be later on.

There are big dogs everywhere. Still, a policeman once told me, following an encounter of mine with a Peeping Tom, that in some situations a noisy little dog can be more valuable than a noisy big one. Little dogs make harder-to-hit targets, is what he told me. Our dog at the time, a far-from-little mutt who usually gave voice even for the passing of a pigeon on the sidewalk, seemed to know this: She had huddled barkless in a corner while the Peeping Tom was around. Maybe that was wise for her, but it wasn't very useful to me. So, wise or not, here is most of the barking I've done, out there with the big dogs. Maybe someone will find it useful.

—*N.B.*, *2014*

Black-line art for duotone illustration in *Phoebe's Revolt* (1969)

"

What, in the very simplest terms, is a child, after all, but an unrepressed adult? What is maturity, that supposed nirvana we seem never fully to achieve, but total emotional control learned from confrontation with experience, which teaches us the necessity for compromise?

"

Happy Endings?
Of Course, and Also Joy

(*1970*)

What in the world is a children's story anyway? What makes it different from a story for adults? Why does one writer choose to write for children and another for adults; or, if you will, what quality makes one writer's work appropriate for children while the work of another points in the other direction?

P. L. Travers has said, "There is no such thing as a children's book. There are simply books of many kinds and some of them children read. I would deny, however, that [they were] written *for* children." Well, perhaps. Sometimes. But someone must have the child in mind even if the author doesn't. Someone, editor or critic, must head a story in the right direction. As a rule, it isn't an especially difficult direction to find. Everyone can tell a child's book from one for adults, just as everyone knows hot water from cold. The difficulty lies in trying to define the essential nature of the difference.

The most common assumption, at least on the part of people who have had little to do with children's literature, is that books for adults are serious in intent while books for children are designed to amuse. But this is only an assumption and nothing more. There are indeed many serious stories for adults and truckloads of children's stories intended only for pleasure, but the reverse is just as true. Fluff, be it trivial or memorable, predominates in both worlds. However, you would be doing both an injustice if you tried to define their separate natures on the basis of fluff. There are no answers to be had by contrasting Jeeves to Winnie-the-Pooh, Hercule Poirot to Nancy Drew, Rhett Butler to the Grinch, or even the Yankee from Connecticut to Dorothy from Kansas. Dear friends all, each in his own place and time, but all members of the same unsubtle family. This leaves in each world an armful of books that are sometimes called classics (make your own list). These are both serious in intent *and* entertaining, as all good stories should be; and it is only in these that any real definition can be found, if in fact it exists at all.

Well, then, perhaps you will say that the difference is still obvious, fluff or no, because adult books deal with adult emotions: love, pride, grief, fear of death, violence, the yearning for success, and so on. But why do we so often forget that children are not emotional beggars? They understand these feelings every bit as well as we do, and are torn by them as often. There is, in point of fact, no such thing as an exclusively adult emotion, and children's literature deals with them all. As for love, "Sleeping Beauty" and her sisters are nothing if not love stories of one kind, while *The Wind in the Willows* is another, and *Heidi* and *Hans Brinker* yet others. Pride? Where is pride more gleefully exposed than in *Toad of Toad Hall*? For grief unsurpassed, try the closing chapters of *The Yearling*. Fear of death begins in childhood and is dealt with supremely well in *Charlotte's Web*, while its other side, the quest for immortality, is dealt with just as well in *Peter Pan*. When it comes to violence, Ali Baba, Jack the Giant Killer, and the brave little tailor are only three of hundreds of inventive and bloody examples. And the yearning for success is a thread so common to all stories that I wonder why I even bothered to bring it up.

There is really no difference where emotional themes are concerned. There are only the subtleties, the nuances, the small ironies, of which adult fiction has made far more use but which are equally available to children's fiction, where their fitness is dictated exclusively by the writer's style and his attitude toward the perceptivity of his readers.

No difference in emotional themes? No—I will correct myself. There is one emotion which is found only in children's literature these years and for many years past, and that emotion is joy.

Next you will perhaps turn to range or scope or whatever you wish to call it. But even here, only at first glance does this appear to be genuine ground for defining a difference. While there was a time when the best adult fiction was timeless in nature and dealt at the core with Everyman, that is no longer true. Decade by decade, new books for adults have become more personal, more singular. It is a long and narrowing road from *Moby-Dick* to *Portnoy's Complaint*. More and more often we find ourselves making do with what Isaac Bashevis Singer has called "muddy streams of consciousness which often reveal nothing but a writer's boring and selfish personality."

Everyman has gone out of fashion for adults. What separates us has come to seem more pertinent than what draws us together. But Everyman is present still in the best children's stories, just as he always has been. All children can identify with and learn from characters like Peter Rabbit and Sendak's Max, in spite of the years between their creation; but many adults have trouble finding common coin with Henry Miller's Mona the way they could with Tolstoy's Natasha.

Content? Barring only graphic sex and other routine adult preoccupations (many of these dull to begin with), there is little difference. War, disability, poverty, cruelty, all the harshest aspects of life, are present in children's literature. Daily banalities are there, too, and the more subtle stuff of boredom, prejudice, and spite. Where did we get the idea that a children's book is gentle and sweet? The only ones that are are those written by people who have been deluded by isolation or a faulty memory into thinking that children themselves are gentle and sweet.

A children's book is peopled with talking animals and other such fantastics? Sometimes, but by no means always. And anyway, adults are just as prone to attributing human characteristics to nonhuman things as children are, in life if not in their fiction. You need only mention the family dog or cat at a dinner party to find this out. And as for the dark world, children did not invent Martians, poltergeists, the séance, or the Devil, or, I might add, the id and the ego, those goblins that out-goblin anything in the Brothers Grimm. If fantasy is absent from adult fiction, it is absent only because adults are too pompous to admit they still have a taste and a need for it.

A children's book uses simple vocabulary geared to the untrained mind? Compare a little Kipling to a little Hemingway and think again. Opening sentence of one chapter from *A Farewell to Arms*: "Now in the fall the trees were all bare and the roads were muddy." Opening sentence of "How the Rhinoceros Got His Skin": "Once upon a time, on an uninhabited island on the shores of the Red Sea, there lived a Parsee from whose hat the rays of the sun were reflected in more-than-oriental splendour." So much for that!

You might in desperation do something with size of type, seeing that children's books are usually printed in larger typeface; but this is really only because they shrewdly refuse to be bothered by anything less. Their eyes, after all, are by and large 20/20 percent better than ours. You might also be reduced to bringing up length—children's books are usually shorter. However, I question whether, having said this, you have said much.

Not one of the above proposals will stand up. They are too arbitrary, too trivial, too riddled with exceptions. Perhaps it is possible only to settle for knowing the difference between the two literatures without being able to articulate it. And there are just enough stories that fall somewhere in between to cloud the issue further. Scrooge, Bilbo Baggins, Alice, Huck Finn, even Charlie Brown—for whom were these created? Ichabod Crane, William Baxter, Jason and Medea, on whose shelf do they belong? Perhaps there is no such thing as a children's book once we are blessedly beyond the forgettable.

And yet it seems to me that there is a tangible difference when you apply one rather simple sieve to the mass. It does not work for every children's story, but perhaps it does apply to all that we remember longest and love best and will keep reading aloud to our children and our children's children as a last remaining kind of oral history, a history of the essence of our own childhood. I am referring, of course, to the Happy Ending.

Not, please, to a simple "happily ever after," or to the kind of contrived final sugarcoating that seems tacked on primarily to spare the child any glimpse of what really would have happened had the author not been vigilant; not these, but to something which goes much deeper, something which turns a story ultimately toward hope rather than resignation and contains within it a difference not only between the two literatures but also between youth and age.

What, in the very simplest terms, is a child, after all, but an unrepressed adult? What is maturity, that supposed nirvana we seem never fully to achieve, but total emotional control learned from confrontation with experience, which teaches us the necessity for compromise? When one learns to compromise, one learns to abandon the happy ending as a pipe dream, or—a children's story.

When we envy our children, we envy them this first of all: "Oh," we say, "they have their whole lives ahead of them," and we believe with them and for them what we no longer believe for ourselves—that anything is possible. We believe that they may grow up to be another Sarah Bernhardt, a Madame Curie, a

Jefferson, a Dickens—pick whichever giant you like. We believe that they may grow up happy, fulfilled, beyond pain. And when we pity our children, we pity them for this: "Oh," we say, "I wouldn't be young and have to go through all that again for anything."

By "all that" we really mean that we remember all too well the first hard lessons in compromise, the abandonment of the primary and then the secondary dream, and so on and on down to what we have at last settled on as possible. Alas, we have arrived and we are not unique after all. We are not beautiful, nor clever, nor even very good; and no matter how well we do what we do, there is always someone who can do it better. The big house on the hill is lost to us forever, and all of our sweet tomorrows are rapidly becoming yesterdays which were almost (if we were lucky) but not quite.

But for the children, no matter how unpromising their circumstances, it is not too late. And we who write for them, or, if you must, we whose work seems appropriate for them, are perhaps those who, far from being glum, have a particularly tenacious view of life as an experiment in possibility without compromise. If we are not clever nor unique, we can at least recall without regret how it felt to believe that we *might* be someday; probably despite plain and discouraging evidence, we are still not totally without hope; and so, in our stories—since, like it or not, every story comes out of the psyche of its author—Wilbur can escape an early death, Cinderella can be queen, Bilbo can outwit the dragon, and the ugly duckling can become a swan. Not without pain, not without violence, not without grief, but in the end, somehow, everything will always be all right.

To be sure, there are stories for adults which end happily, but it is, in the stories that have lasted, a qualified happiness only, the quiet happiness of characters who have made their peace with their own compromises. So Natasha at the end of *War and Peace* "had grown stouter and broader . . . Her features . . . wore an expression of calm softness and serenity. Only on rare occasions now the old fire glowed in her again."

Not so with Ratty and Mole and Toad. Their story ends this way: "The . . . animals continued to lead their lives . . . in great joy and contentment . . . Sometimes, in the course of long summer evenings, the friends would take a stroll together . . . and it was pleasing to see how respectfully they were greeted . . . 'There goes the great Mr. Toad! And that's the gallant Water Rat . . . And yonder comes the famous Mr. Mole . . . !'" Beauty established, nobility achieved, all obstacles overcome. A pipe dream, or—a children's story.

In Nashville, 1960, with Lucy, Chris, and Tom

" *Children are placed outside society, outside useful,* productive *society, to stand with the jet set, hippies, the poor, the aged, and, until recently, women again . . . It is essential at this point to observe how women have traditionally been excluded from the controlling group on many of the same counts as have children, as well as on separate counts.* "

The Child as Chimpanzee

(*1971*)

The world of American children's books has a problem. It's
not a new problem, although it seems more visible these days
than it once did, but it's an awkward problem to define because
we would vastly prefer to deny its existence. However, deny it as
we will, it colors our attitudes in a number of areas of which
children's fiction is only one. To put it flatly, there seems to be a
widespread American belief that children are irrelevant.

As a children's author, one begins to be aware in a dim way
that something is askew when one is asked for the first time, "You
write books for children? But why? How come you don't do something *serious*?" From there one fumbles along, trying hard not to

trip over one's defensiveness, through all the criticism within the field about how there are too many books, and how too many of them are bad, and about how permissive the reviewers tend to be, and how hard the reviews are to find, anyway. And after a time the suspicion begins to grow that the problem itself must be a good deal larger than the sum of these particular parts—that all of them are merely symptoms of a phenomenon which might better be left to the analytic skills of a social psychologist. However, having been offered the opportunity to discuss the current state of children's books, I feel duty-bound to rush in like the proverbial fool and attempt to grapple with the problem itself.

It might be well to begin by looking backward on this belief that children are irrelevant. Consider, then, how as a nation we tend to view all aspects of competence as qualities bestowed, along with the diploma, upon graduation from high school. At that magic moment, the young are ceremoniously separated from the glass through which they have presumably been seeing darkly for eighteen years and—shazam!—they are suddenly become a man. Like so many jovial Saint Peters, commencement speakers across the land welcome them warmly to the heaven of rational adulthood. Even though they may have opted for a stopover in some purgatorial side aisle like the university, they are still counted as among the blessed and are told in ominous tones that they had better act the part. If, through some inexplicable impulse, they should lapse, they are labeled *childish* with a disgust one might suppose was reserved for pejoratives like *leprous* and *treasonous*.

Where have children been before the age of eighteen? What curious, invisible space in society have they been occupying? If the word *childish* is derogatory, does that mean that it is somehow ignoble to be a child? If we are to be honest, we must admit that this is exactly what it means.

For one thing, in a nation where individuals take great pride in the roles they play in their various governments, from the family unit to the White House, children are totally without influence. They stand outside the formal politics of society, along with felons and transients, in an area somewhere beyond the pale where to be cloutless is to be without importance and by extension not worth serious attention, except insofar as children, at least, will eventually "grow out of it" as one "grows out of" acne or asthma.

For another thing, children are small, and this is not as trivial a crime as it may seem. Small people of any age have a hard row to hoe. We have a tendency to look down on those we look down on, as if, Napoleon notwithstanding, length of bone were somehow a yardstick for measuring significance.

Then, too, children are inexperienced. Like the classic job-seeker who has never held a job, they are apt to be denied experience until they have had the experience to handle it. This leads to a curious maze of interconnecting attitudes toward development which culminates in that apron-string-cutting ceremony, the above-mentioned commencement, in which the young are ejected into the world from which they have been scrupulously protected for so long, and expected, by virtue of their sudden attainment of majority, to cope. Until that moment, they have not "set" and are in an unpalatable condition comparable to under-cooked pudding. They are not what they will be, which makes them seem unstable and difficult to deal with.

And finally, as if all this were not enough, children are guilty of the worst crime an American can commit: They are idle. By the rules formulated from the well-known Puritan Ethic, under which we all of us sweat, children are ignoble because childhood is a time of pure pleasure, and pure pleasure is taboo. Never mind that childhood is *not* a time of pure pleasure; according to the Ethic, anyone who is not working must be having fun, and that is a synonym for wasting time. So once again children are placed outside society, outside useful, *productive* society, to stand with the jet set, hippies, the poor, the aged, and, until recently, women again.

Although this is not an article about the condition of women, it is essential at this point to observe how women have traditionally been excluded from the controlling group on many of the same counts as have children, as well as on separate counts. Exclusion carries other stigmas of its own with it, and the most devastating is that nonmembers must by definition be incompetent. In other words, in our society children are the principal responsibility of nonmembers and therefore of incompetents, which says much about their status. The controlling group, turning away from child-raising as "women's work," has tended thereby to class children with *possessions*—a man must have his home, his wife, his children, if he is to be complete. But he participates only marginally in their development, so that children become a facet of home upkeep along with the dish that must be washed and the floor that must be scrubbed—things for someone outside the group to bother about, since group members have other, *serious* work to do. It might also be interesting to observe here how national attitudes toward children's books are exactly parallel to attitudes toward women's magazines: They must be mass-produced for a level of incompetence that cannot absorb anything but trivia.

Given all of this, one might suppose that we would write off children altogether and leave them to their own devices until they reach the "age of reason." But of course we do not do that, for we must willy-nilly see them as tomorrow's citizens, albeit often with dismay, and we are deeply committed to them, but our commitment all too often has a strange flavor consisting of part scorn and part envy: scorn because they must be classed with the Great Excluded, and envy because they can violate the joyless principles of the Puritan Ethic and get away with it, a crime we would all dearly love to commit.

However, the commitment itself, whatever its flavor, remains firm. In this country, giving birth to and rearing children has always been a sacred duty, and for the most part we perform the duty cheerfully enough. The process, after all, fulfills a number of desires and requirements—a road to immortality through re-creation of self, an opportunity for sacrifice and martyrdom, both of which have their own peculiar satisfactions grimly guaranteed by the Ethic, and, not least, that carrot-before-the-nose ideal of creating a better world by improving the race. These are, of course, all perfectly human aspirations; the only trouble with them is that they work more to the advantage of the adult than the child. Since the child is to reproduce and represent the adult, it becomes rather difficult to think of him as a separate and independent entity, to see him in fact as anything but a *potential adult*, a not-yet who is at the same time a shall-be, so that the question is always "What sort of person will you be when you grow up?"—never "What are you now?"

We must, it appears, view children in this light. How else to perpetuate the myth that to be an adult is to be all wise, that the wielder of control is somehow capable to wield? To hint otherwise would be to invite chaos. What is the use of the heaven of our adulthood, that happily-ever-after invented to compensate for the press of responsibility, the fog of compromise, the loss of innocence, the imminence of death—what is the use of it unless we can convince our children, as we were in our turn convinced, that adults are the Best People, worthier than children and inhabiting a better world? We persist, therefore, in the vision of a ladder of life with only two rungs: the bottom rung reserved for children and the top for adults, with nothing in between and no rung at all above adults, by the way, where the aged can rest their bones. And while as adults we allow ourselves certain diversities, children are pressed all together into one vast single child who squats on that bottom rung like a chimpanzee: cute and clever, perhaps, but still only an imitation of humanity.

It has been explained to me that this is the schematic view, a device by which human experience can be ordered. Positions are assigned and lines drawn—such as the proper age for starting school, for voting, for marriage—and by these means we attempt to make sense of the complexities of civilized society, thereby ensuring its continued functioning. The problem is that we have come to accept the abstract scheme as a true description of reality, which it decidedly is not, and this confusion leads to a sharp division between adult and child whereby each is defined in collective terms that often have nothing at all to do with individual realities. Thus adults become tragic, children comic;

adults armored, children vulnerable; adults responsible, children irresponsible; and so on. And the more we compartmentalize, the more tangible the lines between seem to become.

This schism we have created is clearly visible in the vast majority of books we produce for our children, and accounts for the palpable undertone of apology we can discern so often in the words *I write for children.* Having erased the recollection that we were ever children ourselves, or, if not that, then having forgotten what it was really like to be a child—caught up in some eviscerating oversimplification which allows us to recall that our own childhood was entirely pain-free ("Oh, my dear, treasure these years!") or entirely pain-full ("Why, when I was your age," etc. etc.)—we write for them either nothing books or lesson books and miss the mark nine times out of ten.

No one would deny the necessity for many kinds of arbitrary lines between adults and children. Clearly a child of ten is not mature enough for the kind of judgments required, for instance, for educated voting. But while eighteen may do very well as an arbitrary line over which to cross into political maturity—we shall soon see if it will or not—there is no need for arbitrary lines where literature is concerned. A bright ten-year-old might very well comprehend more of *Huckleberry Finn* than a dull sexagenarian. And yet we draw such lines in literature just the same.

People often say to me, "But then, of course, you must limit your vocabulary/insights/tone so that the child will be able to understand." There he is again, the great collective child on the bottom rung of the ladder. But who is he, really, the child? Is he some peculiar creature arrested at age four until suddenly, on commencement day, he is miraculously metamorphosed into a generation of rational adults? Evidently. The best writers for adults write "on the curve," so to speak, knowing perfectly well that their readers will vary—that given the diversity of adult intelligence, there can be layers within layers within layers so that each reader may penetrate as deeply as he can or will. But let *the child's* book be a balloon: one thin, simplistic layer and under that, if he should probe, thin air.

So what is to be done? Children's fiction will never be all that it can be until there is a basic shift in the national attitude toward children themselves. It will have to be a shift which will make it possible for good writers to write for children without suspecting—or being told—that they are somehow prostituting themselves, a shift which will encourage serious critical attention of the same gimlet-eyed variety that is lavished on fiction for adults. Children's fiction must, in other words, be given at least the same level of respectability which child psychology and pediatrics and the manufacture of baby food, among others, now enjoy, with the single difference that these books be allowed to celebrate, as seriously and with as much complexity as they wish, those things which are unique to children as they are, not as they will be, things which are therefore unique in the experience of us all.

In doing this, we would of course have to give up our envy and our scorn and admit that children, in spite of their idleness and their beauty, are something more than mere lilies of the field. We would have to abandon the idea of life as a ladder and re-envision it more realistically as a simple ramp, a ramp to the very top of which none of us ever wishes to travel, since, as in aboriginal concepts of the edges of the Earth, we can only fall off into nowhere when we get there. And once accepting of the ramp image, we would then be forced to acknowledge that we are all continually on the move upward, that no two travel at the same rate of speed, that instead of *the child*, there are children—people who vary at least as much as adults in what they are able to or wish to comprehend. Then, in drawing lines, we would be careful to draw only the necessary ones while at the same time being just as careful not to interpret them as anything but arbitrary.

More than this, we would be forced, with considerable loss to our self-esteem, to admit that adults are not "better" than children, or "worthier"—that we are only as a rule larger and more experienced and a little more tired, with insights that have only replaced other largely forgotten insights. Instead of wondering why an artist of Maurice Sendak's caliber, for instance, should continue to "waste his time" in the field of children's books—and I understand that there are people who wonder—we might then learn to be grateful that there are people like Sendak around who have retained some memory of what the earliest insights were and who are able to communicate that memory in such a way that the gap we have created is closed and the continuum is for a precious moment more real than the schism.

If we do not do these things, it seems clear that all literature will suffer, for it is time we realized that, although Johnny can indeed read, more often than not he doesn't wish to. And who can blame him when his books seem to say that he need only be amused—and if not amused, then at least *occupied*—until the magic moment arrives when he, too, will be the Best People? No wonder his books bore him when we seem to imply in them that he doesn't know a bad one from a good one anyway, so it doesn't matter what he reads—he'll come to the good stuff later on when he's ready; he'll develop a taste for James and Tolstoy and Faulkner and the rest.

It is seriously debatable whether he will develop such a taste. There is a chance, we are told, that literature may disappear. This is the word from the generation that was raised on those little disposable books from the grocery-store rack, the one next to the checkout counter. You know, the books that cost so little it didn't matter if Johnny scribbled in them or tore them up. Remember how cute all those little pictures of kittens were, and those talking garbage trucks?

If literature should die, then we who love it will have helped to kill it. In view of this, it would appear that at the very least we had better learn to include children as respected members at the Thanksgiving feast of all literature instead of relegating them to a midmorning snack. As it now stands, it looks as if we are spoiling their appetites.

Speaking at a convention, 1976

" *We don't take [childhood fears] seriously, however. We resent them, or we laugh at them, or we ignore them altogether, either because we cannot understand them and are therefore afraid of them, or because we do understand them and are therefore afraid of them. The result is that, in the novels we write for children, we write about a world that never existed, not for us when we were young, nor for our present-day young audience. We have, in other words, confused childhood with the good old days.* "

The Great American Novel for Children—and Why Not?

(1973)

Whenever I am asked to talk about children's literature, I always seem to find myself in areas about which I don't know anything really specific and have only my everyday experience to turn to. Writers of fiction form opinions and make statements all the time, heaven knows, but very few of us are scholars. Classicists groan at Robert Graves, historians wince at William Styron, and so on and so on, and I suppose as strong a case can be made against pseudoscholarship in speeches as it can in novels.

Be that as it may, I find it impossible to talk about American children's fiction without stepping squarely into the preserves of sociology and social psychology, though I am not trained in either of those fields. So if there are any scholars of that stripe present here today, I hope they will be generous and allow me to make a number of observations arising out of precisely that—observation—rather than out of any pretense to formal study.

With this apology out of the way, I will pass on fearlessly and begin by assuming that it is acceptable to say there is such a thing as American fiction as a category in the fiction of the world. By this I do not mean merely fiction written by Americans, but one which has a flavor and a thrust distinguishably American, formed from and arising out of all the attitudes, enthusiasms, biases, and eccentricities, all the history past and in the making, all the sophistications and provincialisms that make the United States unique, for better or worse, from other countries.

If you will allow that there is such a thing—an American fiction—I will go on to note that it can itself be divided, in one of many ways, into two categories: one for people under the age of fourteen, and one for people over. Never mind that this division is scarcely into halves; it is a genuine division nonetheless.

Very well. So now we have this category-within-a-category, loosely called American young people's fiction, partaking equally with its counterpart for adults in all those things that are distinguishably American, and, once so defined, it too must be broken down into categories. First there is the picture book, for ages up to eight; then the children's novel for ages eight to twelve; and finally a thing called teenage fiction for ages twelve to fourteen. The age assignments are arbitrary, to be sure, but we've grown accustomed to them, and if they are arbitrary, they are also useful.

The opportunities for creativity presented by each of these three subcategories attract artists of different sorts. The picture book, a very old category, is entirely the bailiwick of illustrators, with the result that though the stories are often weak, the pictures are just as often experimental and exciting, a showcase for developing graphic techniques, and if they are not always a joy forever, still they are certainly things of beauty.

Teenage fiction is a very new category, one which is dominated by our society's shifting definition of what a teenager is and by whatever subject matter the writers suppose will catch the attention of one at any given moment. Since the aberrations of puberty are something no one really understands, least of all those who are going through it, these novels have a hard go trying to order the chaos and must in addition compete with adult novels on the one hand and a widespread impatience with any kind of reading on the other.

Here I will go out on my first limb and suggest to you that in these two categories, picture books and teenage fiction, very little has emerged that properly deserves to be defined as *literature*, if you are willing to accept the definition offered by Van Wyck Brooks when he said, "What makes literature great, of course, is the quality of its subject-matter . . . together with as much formal virtue as the writer is able to compass." Of course, we might all disagree about what that subject matter should be, but Brooks covered the possibilities pretty thoroughly:

> *What makes [works of literature] great is their imaginative force, or their moral force . . . or the size of the arc of life which they subtend . . . their passion*

*for the realities of human nature, or the extent of their
outlook, or the typical or central significance which
their work possesses.*

There are a few picture books which may deserve to be called literature. *The Story of Ferdinand* and *Where the Wild Things Are*, perhaps. But those few are the exceptions that prove the rule. We would not turn automatically to picture books when looking for examples of American *literature*, even if they are all examples of one kind of American fiction.

We would not turn to teenage novels, either. As a category, they are even newer than the group for which they are written, and that is new enough. In addition, they are almost always too much written for the Moment and too narrow in scope to qualify as literature.

However, a *children's novel*, written for the last, best, wisest years of childhood, is something else again. With very few exceptions, this is the traditional, time-proven category into which all of the world's classics for children fall, from *Alice in Wonderland* to *The Little Prince*, and no one would dispute their place in literature. A children's novel is probably the freest of all categories in literature for any age, with the widest range of directions open to the writer, particularly in America, where adult fiction has grown rigid and subjective. And it is dominated by nothing at all, though it has long been the true home of fantasy.

That being so, it would be natural to assume that this category would be enormously attractive and rewarding to serious American writers. But by comparison to the vigorous activity in the other two categories, nothing much has happened in

American children's novels in a very long time, and George Woods, children's book editor of the *New York Times*, has called it something of a wasteland. There is activity, to be sure, if the mere production of published manuscripts can be so described, but that activity lacks vigor, certainly, and on the whole lacks also art, ambition, craftsmanship, and commitment. I base this flat statement in part on my experience as a judge in a well-known book-award contest a couple of years ago for which I read more than ninety books in the children's novel category, all published within a few months of each other and almost all distressingly bad. So it is about this phenomenon and the possible reasons for it that I want to speak. I think there are reasons for it, and I think the reasons are entirely American, typically American, and I also think that the reasons explain why so many of the best children's novels were written somewhere else rather than in America and by Americans.

Some critics, de Tocqueville and Frederick Jackson Turner, for instance, when they commented on the American national character, liked to dwell on its youthfulness. They wrote about the freedom of spirit fostered by the endless frontier, and the strength made possible by the marvelous wealth of the land, and they concluded that these things have led to a certain kind of indomitable spirit kept innocent by continuing success in everything attempted in the way of war, education, agriculture, and commerce.

But other critics, such as Leslie Fiedler, point out that while all that may have been true enough up until the First World War, America has since gone through a series of traumas—the end of the endless frontier, the declining wealth of the land, and wars where no one has been successful—and that these have left her standing disillusioned, resentful, and reluctant on the brink of maturity, all innocence gone and nothing of the old zest left—only a clear and wistful memory of the glory of the good old days when anything was possible.

Indeed, we do seem to cling to the memory of those possibilities, in spite of daily lessons in reality. We are still rushing like lemmings toward our pair of seas, piling up our population on our coastlines, producing for speed and growth when it is clearly no longer necessary. It is impossible to keep us down on the farm. The golden streets beckon; opportunity still knocks.

And yet, in spite of ourselves, we can't really believe in the golden streets and all the rest. Not anymore. And one of the clearest places to find documentation of our disillusionment is in the great American novels of the last sixty years, novels written since the War to End All Wars, which was instead the end of adolescence for our society.

Gloom pervades contemporary novels, and a fine petulance, even a kind of rage. They seem to show an America that has been untimely ripped from the womb of whiz-kid-ism. The rose-colored glasses don't fit so well anymore. And far from accepting the need for a new prescription—bifocals, perhaps—they storm at the necessity to grow and change and age, and they mourn the passing of all the favorite fantasies.

No doubt the discontent these novels present is largely real. Certainly we hide our old people away if they refuse to wear tennis shoes. Certainly we diet and paint and upholster ourselves to look young, men as well as women. Our advertisers tell us over and over that we can stay young if we buy the right products—"You're as young as you feel!"—and they tell us this because it's what we want to hear. Certainly we close our minds to new ideas and to our country as perceived by the truly young, preferring to hold on to what we see as "thinking young" which really means "thinking *before*." For without its youthfulness, how can America be defined?

I have just seen a rather disagreeable movie called *Last Tango in Paris* in which Marlon Brando plays an entirely new breed of American in Paris: middle-aged, lost, half-mad, and entirely unattractive. There are a number of love scenes—well, I guess you couldn't really call them *love* scenes—in which he cavorts with a young French girl. She says she is twenty, and he admits that he is forty-five. In these scenes she is often nude, but he never is. It has been reported that Brando didn't want to be nude in these scenes because he was embarrassed about the condition of his middle-aged body. And yet he was playing the role of a middle-aged man, and any other sort of body would have been a distinct anachronism. So it seems there is a limit to which even our best actors will go in support of the truth.

In any case, we do not like the truth of maturity, or the responsibilities, either. Looking ahead was much more pleasant than the arrival, the past much nicer than the present. If we were Cinderella once, well, so now we're a married woman and so now what?

Our novels give us the answer. Gloom, disappointment, a general disgust with the facts of humanity. Of course it is not all that simple, but still, for novelists, as Brooks observed, "popular success and critical success hinge equally on a low view of the human condition." The great American novel, the serious work of American fiction, must reflect the American view of life, which is essentially disillusioned.

Very well. So now to our children. Now that we know there is no Santa Claus, do we stop insisting that our children believe in him? Quite the contrary! No—American childhood is the last repository of the American dream from which we must all wake after puberty, and we guard it as jealously as we guard our old high school yearbooks. We do this for ourselves, not for our children, since we know perfectly well that we are ensuring for them their own crashing disappointments. But we must see childhood as a time of flawless happiness because that way we have a refuge for our fantasies. We smile mistily when we watch our children happy at their play, and we think how lucky they are. But when they are unhappy, when they are crabby or sad, and when they cry, we grow confused and angry, as if they have let us down. American children get spanked for crying. It is against the rules for them to be anything but apple-cheeked and merry. Those children who never are, those who are deprived in any of a number of ways—in other words, those who are uncooperative enough to be unlucky—we look away from them in embarrassment as if they were bad actors in an otherwise charming play.

The literary result of this game we play with our private truths is easy to see. If adult American novels, to be successful, must reflect the American view of adulthood as essentially disillusioned, children's novels, to be successful, must reflect the American view of childhood as essentially utopian.

But there is something important to remember here: The authors of children's novels are themselves adults, and America's adults all, to a greater or lesser degree, accept the disillusioned view of life. This means that the vast majority of children's authors do not seriously construct a world of promise in their books. Oh, they construct that world, all right, but not seriously. It is nearly always patently artificial, a placebo, lacking one of the essential ingredients literature must possess: consistency with the author's philosophy.

So there is an absence of one kind of honesty in these books, and peripheral to that, an absence of other kinds as well. For the child protagonists of these novels are almost always so one-dimensional that they blow over at the first snort of disbelief. They represent, I suppose, the adult version of untroubled, sterile childhood, a version we cling to in spite of endless studies that suggest the contrary.

Why, good old Dr. Spock, in his commodious pre-protest masterpiece, *Baby and Child Care*, has twenty-five different listings under "Fears" alone, and that stern and practical duo, Gesell and Ilg, in *The Child From Five to Ten*, have written:

> *Life begins with a cry . . . [the newborn baby] cries, on the average, about two hours of each day. This is his most eloquent expressional behavior. We know that babies do not cry without reason. They cry from hunger, pain, discomfort—and also from denials which are not too well understood . . . Many childhood fears seem inconsequential and amusingly absurd. They should, however, always be taken seriously by the adult.*

We don't take them seriously, however. We resent them, or we laugh at them, or we ignore them altogether, either because we cannot understand them and are therefore afraid of them, or because we do understand them and are therefore afraid of them. The result is that, in the novels we write for children, we write about a world that never existed, not for us when we were young, nor for our present-day young audience. We have, in other words, confused childhood with the good old days.

I would like to point out here, however, that the idea is not to present in our novels a world that is one-dimensional in *any* direction. They need be no more entirely gloomy than they should be entirely sunny. The choice is not between Pollyanna and the Pit. Gesell and Ilg go on to say that

> *good stories . . . provide fear experiences that enlarge the child's imagination. Literature, like life, introduces him to pain and evil and helps him in the task of surmounting both.*

But Gesell and Ilg would no doubt agree that literature, like life, has more facets than merely the dark ones.

Still, we want to avoid sharing the dark ones with our children. We dare not. It would destroy something precious in them, we think, and, by association, in us. We have made them the keepers of the myth, and the myth is sacred. If, when they reach adolescence, we let them have the disillusioned view right between the eyes, well, we say, they're ready for it. We make them a present of it both as a reward for their arrival and as a swift apology for our previous pretension.

I submit to you that if the world as depicted in American children's novels is sweet beyond bearing, the world of American adult novels is black beyond reason, and where the two come together, in teenage fiction, the world is melodramatic almost to the point of surrealism. And the whole range is pointlessly mirthless and entirely subjective.

It might be helpful if, instead of sitting about contemplating our national navel, we looked outward for a change. America, after all, is not the world, though, disillusioned or not, we still feel that it is the best part of the world. And while it would be impossible for novels written by Americans not to reflect to a preponderant degree things American—impossible and certainly undesirable—still, it would be refreshing if our novels could reflect also something more. We are, after all, first and foremost, members of the human race, and therefore we have much in common with the rest of the world and much to learn from it.

To be sure, we have expended a good deal of effort in trying to establish our own personal literature. It wasn't easy. In fact, it has been observed that American literature has only been "self-perpetuating and self-sustaining" since about 1850. If this is a date impossible to pin down, still it came about, however gradually, not so very long after Ralph Waldo Emerson, speaking before the Phi Beta Kappa Society in Cambridge in 1837, said sternly, "We have listened too long to the courtly muses of Europe."

So ours is a young literature and we should be proud of what we have accomplished. But perhaps it is time to turn a corner, to grow up, for Brooks has said that American literature is still "immature." Perhaps we should try to get past these polar views of life-as-disillusionment and life-as-utopia, and admit in our novels, for whatever age, that it is neither and both, a fine mixture that needs interpreters who are objective, not subjective, and who, though certainly serious, are still mature enough not to be so boringly mirthless.

John Barth, one contemporary American novelist for adults who, in my opinion, fits the needed mold, gives one of his characters, in his splendid book *The Sot-Weed Factor*, the following speech:

> *We sit here on a blind rock careening through space; we are all of us rushing headlong to the grave. Think you the worms will care, when anon they make a meal of you, whether you spent your moment sighing wigless in your chamber, or sacked the golden towns of Montezuma? . . . We are dying men . . . i'faith, there's time for naught but bold resolves.*

If *The Sot-Weed Factor* is a great American novel, and I think it is, and if it happens to be neither glum nor beamish, but rather matter-of-fact—if, in other words, it departs in interesting ways from Brooks's dictum that success for novels hinges on a low view of the human condition, and yet if it still manages to be polled by *Book Week* as one of the best American novels since 1945— why then should not novelists for children aspire to be the John Barth of the children's world? Why, instead of acquiescing to the popular view that our novels must be sugarcoated lies—and therefore non-literature—can we not make our own bold resolves and write novels that discard utopia and hell alike, interpreting instead the real ambivalent world to children as human beings, with as much honesty and skill as we can muster?

You will think from this, perhaps, when I speak about the

real ambivalent world, that I am saying we must talk straight from the shoulder, give the kids the facts, no more fantasy, no more magic, no more fun. No. I am saying that we should use the language in all its infinite richness and variety, and use our imaginations in all the freedom that the medium allows, to tell stories that illuminate both for us *and* our young audience our common human roots. If we can find a way to look at childhood as we knew it ourselves to be, to cut through the cloud of half myth, half amnesia that so often distorts our view, then we can write and communicate honestly and seriously. Not in a loud voice and with a barbered vocabulary as if we were speaking to someone who does not *understand* the language. And certainly not as moralizing old fuddy-duddies. What do *we* know, after all? We are all on this "blind rock careening through space," and children who are old enough to read children's novels are well aware of the fact. They have their own metaphors, to be sure, but we have access to those metaphors. They are, in fact, more universal than our own. Fantasy in particular is ancient, common ground, and one of the most fruitful ways of interpreting and ordering fact. I am talking, however, about Tolkien's brand of fantasy, not the grocery-store-book variety. The difference is the difference between literature and blather, between a searchlight and a blindfold, between a magic carpet and a bath mat.

We can, in other words, aspire to create literature. Any kind of writing is hard work, so why not try to have something worthwhile to show for it? There is no reason why children's authors should have to serve up the sherbet of the literary feast and then be forced to apologize to our colleagues in the adult world because our creations melt on touch. We have had so little respect for our work that we do not even do it carefully, and many of our own editors, critics, and reviewers allow us to get away with sloppiness that could never pass in novels for adults. No wonder American children's novels have a questionable literary reputation. Sloppy craftsmanship, sloppy philosophy, all okay so long as it is colored Pepto-Bismol pink. This is not art. As Anthony Burgess wrote in a recent article, "Art that merely soothes is not art at all; it may even be thought of as anti-art . . . Anti-art dulls awareness; art enhances it."

Why should we not aspire to enhance the awareness of our children? I refuse to believe that we do not have it in us to tell tales that can be works of literature—works of art—and American, and for children, all at the same time, if we are willing to fly in the face of what is after all a very young sacred cow. It is necessary to be hopeful to write successfully for children, yes, because children themselves are generically hopeful, but the quality of hopefulness is not an *immature* quality. Quite the contrary. If it is something we have abandoned in our adult literature, that is one of the reasons why that literature remains immature. Despair is not a philosophy; it is a whine, a fashion, and a boring one at that.

So there is work to be done. We are only just beginning. There is a wasteland to be irrigated, and who knows what fine stuff can be grown there? It would be very good to get down on our hands and knees and work in real soil and raise real plants, the very best we are capable of, knowing we don't have to conjure up some plastic representation of a flowering Eden which must, for the sake of an underrated audience, remain forever serpentless. And how nice for that audience to be respected at last—readers who won't have to undergo the silly and needless trauma of expulsion from some plastic literary Eden straight into an equally plastic literary hell. We can instead give our children great books—we can give them *literature* if we really want to, if we are willing to sweat a little and get our hands dirty. Just think of it! The great American novel for children! Why not?

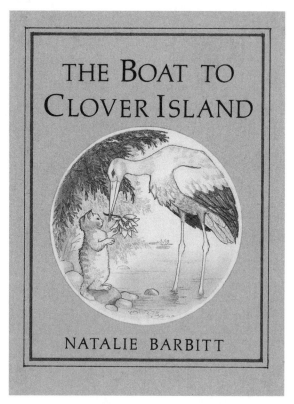

THE BOAT TO
CLOVER ISLAND

NATALIE BARBITT

Babbitt's cover mock-up for an unpublished manuscript.
"I ran out of Bs," the author notes to her editor in the
margin of the design.

*I couldn't make the story work because, among other reasons, the charac-
ters should, I knew, have been animals from the beginning—old animals
who were turned back into young animals by the stork. But I find it exceedingly difficult to write about talking animals. I like to* read *stories that
have talking animals in them, but I can't seem to write such stories.*

You Must Go Home Again

(*1978*)

All of us writers and readers of fantasy are in a trap, have always been in a trap, and there's no escape. I didn't know this until a few years ago. Of course, there were hints. For instance, I often wondered why it seemed so essential to take the young heroes and heroines of my stories away from their bed and board and send them out alone into the world to have their adventures. It was very hard, and is very hard, to keep inventing reasonable excuses for separating them from their parents. You can't go on forever making orphans of them—it's tiresome and it doesn't always make sense. But beyond grumbling over this single problem, I didn't recognize the trap for what it was until one day in 1972.

I had been working for nearly a year on a story which refused to be good. It was about a group of people, staying at a lakeside summer hotel, whose lives were all stalled in one way or another. They had lost their dreams and hopes and were not enjoying themselves very much. Each one had the physical characteristics of a different animal, and a name to match (Eunice Woolsey Merino, for instance, was a woman who was a whole lot like a sheep), but each had forgotten how to appreciate life on the simple, innocent level of young animals or, if you will, children. In the course of the story, each was turned into the animal he was most like, and carried off by a character called the Animal Man (who himself had turned into a stork) to a small abandoned island just offshore from the hotel, where, when they were all assembled, they remembered their childhood and their dreams and were refreshed into a happier, more hopeful view of the future.

I couldn't make the story work because, among other reasons, the characters should, I knew, have been animals from the beginning—old animals who were turned back into young animals by the stork. But I find it exceedingly difficult to write about talking animals. I like to *read* stories that have talking animals in them, but I can't seem to write such stories. Nevertheless, it seemed to me to be a good idea, the whole notion of rebirth by means of a stork and a magic island set apart from the world where one could recapture one's original innocence and joy and then come back to the real world restored to one's physical self, but emotionally refreshed and renewed. It seemed to me to be such an original idea, the separation problem for its child hero solved by giving her a trip to the hotel with an aunt who was keeping her while her mother had a new baby. Birth again! The fact that the story was ultimately a failure is beside the point here. The key thing is the excitement I felt over its ingredients: the magic island, the stork who carried people there, the whole idea of renewal and return.

During the same period I had been reading Roald Dahl's book *James and the Giant Peach*, urged on me by one of my children. It was a splendid story, I thought, but there was something the matter with the way it ended. I couldn't figure out exactly what bothered me, though, and since I was working on my own troublesome story, I forgot about James.

Then, on that fateful day in 1972, a student of mine gave me a book she had been reading in a philosophy course. It was called *The Hero with a Thousand Faces*, and the author was a man named Joseph Campbell. My student was very excited about the book. Spurred by her enthusiasm, I sat down and began to flip through its pages. And as I did so, my eye lit on a few lines at the end of the first chapter:

> *This first stage of the mythological journey—which we have designated the "call to adventure"—signifies that destiny has summoned the hero and transferred his spiritual center of gravity from within the pale of his society to a zone unknown. This fateful region of both treasure and danger may be variously represented: as a distant land, a forest, a kingdom underground, beneath the waves, or above the sky, [or it may be] a secret island . . .*

I was dumbfounded. What had I done? Had I somehow forgotten a story I had once read that had a secret island in it exactly like mine? A zone unknown to which a character was summoned? Was I a closet plagiarist? So I began to read the book in earnest, and that is how I discovered, to my delight and annoyance, the trap I told you about a few moments ago.

There is no point in trying to explain in any detail what *The Hero with a Thousand Faces* has to say. It is a dense, scholarly work which has finally more to do with religion, and particularly Buddhism, than it does with the writing of fantasy. There are large portions which I had great difficulty in following. And it never even mentions children's literature (except for the classic fairy tales, which after all were not created for children alone). But the gist is simple enough.

The book shows that the fantasy hero and his adventures are universal to all cultures, and the ancient path he follows, though it leaves room for certain variations of detail, is in the main unalterable and inescapable. In Campbell's own words: "The standard path of the mythological adventure of the hero is . . . separation, initiation, return." Once you understand the pattern, you see it everywhere in all fantasy literature, as well as in classic myth. As I trace it for you, I'll use *Peter Pan*, *The Wizard of Oz* (Baum's version, and also Hollywood's), and *Alice in Wonderland* for examples. That will help in showing how the pattern emerges.

The hero's story begins with a "call to adventure," usually from a character of some sort which Campbell calls "the herald." The herald can be ugly or beautiful, frightening or attractive or odd, but whatever form it takes, it summons the hero to cross a threshold from the real world into mystery, from life into death, from the waking state into dream. For Campbell, these are all one and the same threshold. For Alice, the herald is the White Rabbit, and she leaves her sister's side to follow him down the rabbit hole. For Wendy and Michael and John, Peter Pan himself is the herald. For Dorothy the herald takes the nonhuman form of a cyclone.

"Once having traversed the threshold," says Campbell, "the hero moves in a dream landscape . . . where he must survive a succession of trials." But he will be assisted by some kind of protective figure who will give him charms to help him in his struggles. For Alice, there are a number of these protective figures, but the Caterpillar is the most obvious: He gives her the hint about the sides of the mushroom which will eventually make it possible for her to get through the tiny door into the beautiful garden. For Wendy and her brothers, Peter Pan, in addition to being the herald, is the protector as well. For Dorothy, it is the Good Witch of the North who starts her on her way and provides the charm: the mark of a kiss on her forehead. (In the book there are no ruby slippers—only silver ones, the magical qualities of which are unknown.) And Dorothy has beside her throughout the story the very protective Scarecrow, Tin Woodman, and Cowardly Lion.

If it were not for these protective figures or devices, which Campbell calls symbols of "the benign, protecting power of destiny," the hero would never be able to survive the trials of his adventures to come. And though in every story the trials are different, they all represent, according to Campbell, a coming face-to-face with the confusions, terrors, and pains hidden in the hero's subconscious mind, that stand between him and the achievement of spiritual perfection.

This concept can best be described, where children's fantasy literature is concerned, as the lesson the hero must learn before he can become an adult. It takes many forms, that lesson, and in *Alice in Wonderland* it is very difficult to see it clearly at all, for though Alice's adventures are full of trials, there is no overt lesson to be learned. For Wendy and her brothers, the lesson is clear, though it is the author's lesson, not Peter's: When the time comes to grow up, it's best to do it and leave childhood behind. And for Dorothy, the lesson is equally clear, though Hollywood spells it out differently from Baum: The real lesson here is that we can control our own destinies if we want to. As Russell MacFall says in *To Please A Child*, his biography of Baum, "What we want, [Baum] the moralist whispers, is within us; we need only look for it to find it. What we strive for has been ours all the time."

Having survived the trials, then, and learned the lesson, the hero is free to return to the real world or the waking state or life—however you wish to define it—to recross the threshold, bringing with him his new knowledge. In classical myth, this knowledge, what he has learned in that other place, may be used to enlighten the world. But sometimes the knowledge, or "boon," as Campbell calls it, is too difficult or too bizarre to be understood by ordinary people. "How [can the hero] communicate," he says, "to people who insist on the exclusive evidence of their senses, the message of the all-generating void? . . . Why attempt to make plausible, or even interesting, to men and women consumed with passion, the experience of transcendental bliss?" Dorothy makes no attempt to explain Oz to Auntie Em on her return, and even in Hollywood's version, though she does try, the people around her don't believe her and she soon gives up the effort. Wendy and Michael and John are likewise silent, though their mother, Mrs. Darling, would have understood Neverland very well indeed. Alice, on the other hand, gets around the problem quite easily: She calls her adventures a dream, and as we all know, anything can happen in dreams. Tolkien has said that *Alice in Wonderland* is not a true fantasy, since it dismisses the adventures this way. He claims that in true fantasy, the world across the threshold is as real on its own level as the everyday world we inhabit, and continually coexists with it. But Campbell would say, I think, that it doesn't matter that Alice calls her adventures a dream; for him, dreams, myth, and fantasy are all the same world, all using the same symbols to the same ends.

Where does all this—the pattern of the classic hero's path—leave the writer of fantasy? Once Campbell spelled it out for me, I could understand why I was trapped into separating my child heroes from their parents: I was following a route laid down thousands of years ago. It was strong in my subconscious, even though I didn't know it. Adventure means exposure, danger, and growth, and there can be very little of that if parents are present. They have to be done away with, kept out of sight, left behind, if anything interesting is going to happen. They belong to one reality while the adventure belongs to another. And on top of that, they are symbols of overprotection, and can retard development. The hero cannot grow if he is shielded from the very elements which create growth. So acceptance of the call to adventure represents the great rite of separation, the cutting of the apron strings.

One does not have to cross the threshold into adventure and danger all alone. Hansel and Gretel have each other. In *Charlie and the Chocolate Factory*, Charlie Bucket takes along his grandfather. Sometimes, as in *The Wizard of Oz*, the young hero will take an animal along. In the immortal words of Hollywood's Wicked Witch of the West: ". . . and your little dog, too." But the hero never takes a parent along. The apron strings, which are a symbol for the umbilical cord, are severed forever when the call to adventure is answered.

After this, the hero's path is clear. He has his trials, survives them, receives his boon or learns his lesson, and then returns to the real world. And seeing this final step, I knew at once why the ending of *James and the Giant Peach* was disturbing to me: James goes to a magic world and stays there, rather than returning. That is a violation of the pattern, a remaining in the dream state, the death state, a rejection of the notion of rebirth. In myth, in dream, in fantasy, if you are the hero, you must leave the real world, you must face and successfully complete your trials, and then, with your newfound knowledge in hand, you must go home again. In every case, home, though it is safer, is less attractive than the other world. Kansas, compared to Oz, is a wasteland. London, compared to Neverland, is dull. And sitting under a tree being read to by your sister is far less exciting than being in Wonderland. Nevertheless, if you are the hero, home is where you have to go.

Campbell would say that all of us know the pattern well without having to be taught. We were born with an understanding of it, subconsciously, and everything that happens in our lives reinforces it. But for most of us, certainly for me, it remains subconscious until it is somehow exposed. I've told you that *The Hero with a Thousand Faces* is a densely scholarly work. I can't keep much of its wealth of detail in my head for long at a time. I read it first in 1972 and then again this past winter. In between, I wrote several stories, including one called *Tuck Everlasting*. Imagine my chagrin on coming across the following passage in *Hero* this winter, one I must have read six years ago, in the chapter dealing with that first step, the call to adventure:

> *Typical of the circumstances of the call are the dark forest, the great tree, the babbling spring, and the loathly, underestimated appearance of the carrier of the power of destiny.*

Some of you may have read *Tuck Everlasting*. If so, you will recall my own dark forest, great tree, babbling spring, and my own loathly carrier, or herald, Winnie Foster's toad. I had a letter from a child last week asking me why I put a toad into this story. How can I give a simple answer? The toad is there because my subconscious told me I had to supply my hero with a herald? But that is the only true answer.

It is annoying in the extreme to find that one's work, struggled with for so long, and finally finished after trying and discarding numberless bits of detail, can be found to have been summed up—parts of it, anyway—by a scholar years before one even began, and described as "typical." I knew my ash tree and spring were ancient symbols of immortality and I used them for that very reason, but I didn't know, consciously, that for this story they were representing any kind of threshold. And I certainly didn't like to think of them as preordained and typical. I didn't and don't like to think that I have so little freedom of choice, that the pattern with all of its elements laid out is so deeply instilled in me that it leads me without my knowing I am being led.

Still, we have to come to the conclusion that all fantasy stories are fundamentally alike. Their patterns are immutable, and as writers we must follow them willy-nilly or suffer the consequences of a plotline gone askew. It is annoying, but it is miraculous, too. We are trapped, but it is a kind of confinement that makes a brotherhood of us all, writers and readers alike, here, everywhere, and on back to our common prehistory ancestors. For the questions have never changed, and the answers are always the same.

Carl Sagan, in his remarkable book *The Dragons of Eden*, talks at length about the two halves of the brain—everyone's brain: how the left side is the residence of logic and language, while the right side is the home of dream and intuition and creativity. Much of the truth of this brain division has been established through surgical experiments on animals, and observance of human accident victims. But Sagan goes on beyond facts and into theory to talk about the content of the brain's right side. The logical left side tries hard to control and repress the intuitive right side, but in sleep the left relaxes its vigil and the right brings images up to the surface that in the waking state would never be permitted. Sagan quotes Erich Fromm at this point. Fromm, he says, calls these images "the forgotten language" and "argues that they are the common origin of dreams, fairy tales, and myths." Whether or not these images are common to all of us, whether or not there is such a thing, really, as "race memory," may be arguable. But I believe with Sagan that we do all ask the same urgent questions and fear the same implacable monsters. There is no other way to explain the remarkable similarity among the world's myths of creation, for instance, as well as among its wealth of folk and fairy tales.

The common questions, put simply, seem to be: Who am I? What is the meaning of life? Can I make my way through it alone? And must death be the final end? We all begin, after all, in the same way: We are protected by our parents for a time, and then we are thrust out into the world without them. Sometimes there are happy ceremonies to mark this thrusting out—ceremonies like bar mitzvahs or graduations or weddings—and sometimes the event is unceremonious and harsh. But it must take place if we are to grow. Still, the world is dangerous, and most of us are afraid as we head out into it alone. We wonder if we are strong enough. But we face our trials as bravely as we can, and most of us, fortunately, can say to ourselves, as the theme song of *The Mary Tyler Moore Show* says to its hero, "You're going to make it after all." We must all follow the mythic hero's path, and his experiences have for centuries served as a guide for us, whether we realize it or not.

Throughout the struggle, however, no matter how successful we are, we still fear the ultimate separation, death. In myths and fairy tales, the heroes seldom die a literal death within the bounds of the story, but their happy endings are not denials of death. Happy endings, says Campbell in his *Hero with a Thousand Faces*, are "to be read not as a contradiction, but as a transcendence of the universal tragedy of man." In myth and fairy tale, death is dealt with symbolically. Snow White and Sleeping Beauty are both awakened from their long sleeps—for which read: resurrected from their deaths—by the kiss of a prince, and are carried off to the typical fairy-tale heaven of a castle where it is possible to live happily ever after. In much of children's fantasy literature, this last step to the hero's final reward will take place, as I have said, beyond the scope of the story, but we know that some kind of heaven awaits him, for he has completed his trials successfully and has earned that final reward. For my own Tuck family, the final reward is withheld, but Winnie, the standard hero, achieves it fully.

So how do we explain Peter Pan? He is a herald announcing the call to adventure, and a protector of Wendy and her brothers, but he is also a hero himself, a hero who has refused to take the final step and return to the real world, to adulthood and eventual death. He has chosen instead to remain forever in Neverland, having the same adventures over and over again, and he tries hard to persuade Wendy and the Lost Boys to do the same. Barrie makes it clear, however, that there is a heavy price to pay for refusing to return: One forfeits all rights to putting one's learned lessons, or "boons," to work in the real world. To remain a child, though it has advantages, nevertheless means that you will remain immature, ignorant, powerless, and unfulfilled.

These facts apply as well to James in *James and the Giant Peach*. But he and Peter Pan are not unique. Campbell points out that the return is often refused in myth and folklore. "The full round," he says, "requires that the hero . . . [come] back into the kingdom of humanity, where the boon may redound to the renewing of the community, the nation, the planet, or the ten thousand worlds." And when the hero refuses to complete the round, he has, in fact, chosen to withdraw from his own humanity.

It would be well nigh impossible to name a single fantasy or fairy tale where the pattern or some major portion of it does not prevail. Whether the call to adventure is heralded by Pinocchio's Cat and Fox, or Charlie Bucket's golden ticket, or the appearance of Mary Poppins, there will be a herald of some kind, always. Whether the threshold is Alice's rabbit hole, or the desert surrounding Oz, or the closet in the Narnia series, there will be a threshold always. Whether the protective charm is as simple as Cinderella's fairy godmother or as complex as the usual youngest son's usual three objects given him by the usual hag he encounters on the road, there will always be some kind of charm. Adventures and trials will always be present, for they form not only the conflict and suspense of the story, but more important, they represent the struggle to learn the necessary lesson and achieve the mastery of one's own fears. As for coming home again, where it happens, there is a completion of the round and a feeling of satisfaction. And where there is a refusal to return, there is the suggestion that for the particular hero of the particular story, reality is not worth returning to. For most, however, the ending will be happy.

Why, if the patterns of fantasy are so unchangeable, do writers of fantasy not get tired of it? Well, I, for one, *do* get tired of it and sometimes wish for more elbow room to explore my ideas. The trouble is, I believe in the pattern. It's the only kind of story line that seems to make any final kind of sense. And this means that I believe in happy endings. Modern adult fiction, and much of what we call teenage fiction, cannot itself entirely escape the pattern; the difference is that in much of this type of fiction, the hero will refuse the call in the first place, or worse, he will cross the threshold only to be defeated in his trials, or to opt for remaining in that other world. This, for instance, is the principal difference between the movies *Star Wars* and *Close Encounters of the Third Kind*. *Star Wars* is a classic fantasy with the hero's round complete. *Close Encounters* is a modern study: The hero, after struggling through most of the story merely to answer the call to adventure, crosses the threshold only at the end, and the implication is that the round, which took so long to begin, will never be completed—the hero will not come home again.

For me and for all writers devoted to fantasy as a means of exploring ideas, the total round of the hero's path is vitally important. We cannot tell stories that satisfy us without it. And I think there will always be a place for us in the world of fiction. There always has been for as long as the basic, simple questions have been asked. Fantasy will continue to answer those questions symbolically at some level and in some place that is always unexplained and yet universally understood. In *The Dragons of Eden*, Carl Sagan quotes a fourth-century philosopher, Sallustius: "Myths are things which never happened, but always are." To carry on in that tradition, to take the hero through his round and bring him home again, over and over, is a tradition that will never lose its vitality or its value. I hope that in these practical times, with their new and urgent practical problems, you will agree with me that while we must, with realistic fiction, define and redefine for our children our rapidly changing physical world, we also have an obligation to serve the needs of their ancient, searching, universal souls.

Ralph Moore with his two daughters, Natalie (standing) and Diane, 1940

I suppose I was word-conscious at an early age because, though we weren't
scholars, we were nevertheless word people. My father loved puns and jokes
and could make us laugh over and over again at the same things.

Saying What You Think

(*1981*)

S omeone said once that the older we get, the more aware we
are that we don't know much, and that's all right—I don't
have any quarrel with that. But the trouble is, it's also true that
the older we get, the more we're expected to sound as if we know
a great deal.

It took me a long time to accept the idea that I *had* to know
things, in the first place, and even longer to accept the idea that
I would from time to time have to explain what I knew, and even
longer than that to realize that what I knew was more than likely
going to be challenged by someone who knew something else

altogether. That can be very intimidating if you haven't had much practice. There's nothing so hard to defend as an opinion.

I had a lot of opinions when I was a child, hundreds and hundreds, but was almost never asked to defend them. Then, later on, I went through a period when I had no opinions at all. After that came a stretch when I had three or four opinions but was mostly too timid to articulate them and even less able to defend them when challenged. I have in the last fifteen years arrived at a stage where I have, oh, maybe as many as a dozen opinions, all tried and true, and I can defend every one if I have to. What's more, I don't care anymore whether anyone agrees with me or not. I am not even alarmed when I meet someone who has maybe as many as fifty or sixty opinions. As you know, a person with fifty or sixty opinions lives an easier life than the rest of us. Decisions are a snap; judgments can be reached in the wink of an eye; the mind is as easy to make up as a daybed. But now when I am confronted by someone like that, I can listen with comparative calm, and, while I'm listening, I just take out one of my own opinions and roll it around in my head without bothering anyone about it, and it's very reassuring. One opinion of mine that is very good for this purpose, an opinion so old it's way back at number two on my list, is that *The Water-Babies* by Charles Kingsley is a silly book.

I can defend that opinion, chapter and verse, to anyone who wishes to challenge it. But I couldn't always. *The Water-Babies* was, after all, one of the books on my mother's list of children's classics—a list put out by persons unknown—and by the time my sister and I were through with grammar school, she had read every one of them aloud to us.

I remember being alarmed by parts of *Hans Brinker* and *Heidi*, and we never heard the ending of *The Yearling* because my mother couldn't get through it without weeping. *Robinson Crusoe* was a little dull, and, as I've said, *The Water-Babies* was silly. And I was left pretty much untouched by *Robin Hood, Peter Pan*, and a number of others. But I loved *Alice in Wonderland, Penrod*, and most of the *Just So Stories*. Except for *Alice*, the illustrations in these books had nothing at all to do with what I liked or didn't like. And I don't think the stories themselves had as much to do with it as you might expect. It seems to have had mainly to do with the language used—whether or not it was funny, unusual, and evocative. And so when Charles Kingsley said in *The Water-Babies* that "Tom was always a brave, determined little English bull-dog, who never knew when he was beaten," I was not amused.

I suppose I was word-conscious at an early age because, though we weren't scholars, we were nevertheless word people. My father loved puns and jokes and could make us laugh over and over again at the same things. And I think he made an effort to make his own speech fresh and funny. We laughed often and easily, but I soon learned that whether or not a thing seems funny has much to do with the circumstances under which it's heard and who is doing the speaking. My friends almost never thought the things my father said were funny when I repeated them.

I think my friends thought my family was a little weird, and I guess in a lot of ways we were. I suppose that's why my father's mother and James Thurber's mother were such good friends while my father was growing up in Columbus, Ohio. The Thurbers, as we all know from stories like "The Night the Bed Fell," were not exactly run-of-the-mill, and though my father never knew James Thurber—they went to different schools—he did remember often coming home to find his mother and Mrs. Thurber sitting in rocking chairs on the front porch. Mrs. Thurber always seemed to be telling a funny story, rocking back and forth, slapping her knees and laughing.

You wouldn't think offhand that there could be anything particularly fertile for the antic imagination about growing up in Columbus, but maybe people were funny in self-defense. Of course, one man's funny is another man's weird. My father's family was unusual, to put it mildly. But *he* thought they were funny, and so, of course, we did, too. I would dearly love to tell stories about them, but that would take us far afield from the topic at hand, so I will discipline myself and say instead that the point in all this is that I had a tendency to like books that seemed to me to have a way with words. The stories themselves didn't have to be funny, necessarily, but they certainly had to be diverting, and they had to have a hero with whom it would be nice to change places. I don't think I thought very much about content or the thrust of an argument. I don't recall our ever discussing that aspect. But occasionally it was so obvious that it hit you in the face. That was one of the troubles with *The Water-Babies*. The whole family disliked *The Water-Babies*, though we dutifully read it all the way through. I am much gratified by the fact that it doesn't seem to be required anymore.

Beyond this—the congenial hero and the language—I remember being beguiled by the environment in which a story was read. We read aloud more often in the summers, particularly during my father's vacations, when we would sit in a cushioned swing hung in a corner of the screened porch of my mother's mother's cottage at a place called Indian Lake in northwestern Ohio. It was lovely to curl up there beside my mother on a hot afternoon and listen to stories. It would have been almost impossible to dislike any author's works—except Charles Kingsley's—under those circumstances; the entire ambiance was so charming. My father was always off blissfully fishing, or about to go blissfully fishing, or just coming back from blissfully fishing; my grandmother seemed always to be in the kitchen either baking a pie or making a kind of candy we had a fondness for, which in hindsight seems truly ghastly, since its sole ingredients were powdered sugar, cold mashed potatoes, and peanut butter. And the amusement park across the road was always in full swing, so that the narrative my mother was reading was punctuated by the gradual crescendo and diminuendo of the roller coaster and the shrieking of its happy victims. It was a backdrop Lewis Carroll would have understood and thoroughly approved of, in fiction if not in life.

The books we read by ourselves were not on my mother's list, but she didn't seem to mind. My sister preferred to go off alone, up in a tree if there was a good one near by, and cry over *Little Women* or *Uncle Tom's Cabin*, while I ate oranges in my bedroom and read fairy tales. And in the evenings my father read Arthur Conan Doyle's *The White Company* and Rafael Sabatini novels over and over again, as well as every detective story he could get his hands on. Curiously, I don't remember my mother reading to herself at all, though I suppose she must have.

But I want you to understand that we didn't talk about books. We simply enjoyed them or didn't enjoy them, the way we enjoyed or didn't enjoy eating depending on the menu. Books were a normal part of our daily lives, and beyond the list of children's classics, no one told us we *should* read such and such, or *shouldn't* read so and so. We were entirely unselfconscious about it.

And then, during her adolescence, my sister suddenly developed another point of view about reading. I'm not sure how it began. But all at once she was plowing through very difficult books—or so they seemed to me—and though she didn't force them on me or our parents, still she seemed to me to be expressing silent but palpable disapproval of my fairy tales and my father's whodunits. Some of her new tastes may have been implanted by a series of curmudgeonly English teachers in high school, but however it began, she was soon off in corners every night reading Faulkner and Melville—the days for reading aloud being largely over—while my mother and I played a word game called anagrams. Looking back, I know she loved those books and I understand why, but at the time, since she never laughed aloud or even smiled while she was reading, I couldn't understand what she saw in them. But she was a straight-A student—a hard and conscientious worker—while I avoided everything that didn't come easily, so I wrote off her new reading habits as the tiresome behavior of a grind and began to devour my father's Sabatinis, which I assure you I enjoyed very much indeed.

Needless to say, knowing what we now know about sibling rivalry, my preferences were no doubt partly dictated by a strong desire to identify myself in opposition to my sister, but it is just as true that a lot of my distaste for the books I had to read in school had to do with the way they were presented. They were homework, while the reading I did on my own was fun.

I discovered a lot of books on my own, outside of school and college, books that, had they been assigned to me by a teacher, might well have seemed just as painful as *Oliver Wiswell* and *Tess of the d'Urbervilles.* I read Tolstoy and Dreiser and Dickens and Sinclair Lewis, and a number of others too dubious to mention, and found them wonderful, and was launched on a bad habit I still have of discovering an author and proceeding to read straight through the entire oeuvre without a pause. This is a bad habit because a writer's devices and biases soon begin to stick out, and his work becomes predictable by the time you're into the third or fourth novel. Still, the point is, I read for the great pleasure it gave me but never really talked about it to anybody.

I married, after college, a man who was in the process of acquiring a PhD in American studies with a concentration in American literature. I didn't marry him for his PhD, but rather for a number of other reasons having more to do with fun. And a good thing, too, since we didn't at all have the same taste in books. One day early in our marriage I had been reading something or other and said enthusiastically that I liked it, and this man I had married turned a shrewd professorial eye on me and said, "Why?"

Believe it or not, all through twelve years of school and four years of college, no one had ever asked me that question. I had been led and sometimes dragged through large numbers of works I have comfortably forgotten, without my own opinion about them ever having been solicited. The stories we read aloud at home we either liked or didn't like, but we never talked about *why*. And in school, if the teacher or professor thought a writer was important, who was I to contradict in exams and term papers? You gave the professors what they wanted, and what they wanted was not your opinion, but your acceptance of *their* opinion. At least, that is what I remember.

And anyway, I was vaguely ashamed of not liking writers like Thomas Hardy and William Faulkner. And that is important, I think, that sense of shame. We are fond of assuming that children are so unselfconscious and direct that they can always be depended on to point out that the emperor has no clothes on. *Some* children are unselfconscious and direct, for a *while*. But they get it pounded out of them. We all learn pretty quickly that honesty is not always the best policy when it comes to such hard-to-defend areas as opinions. On the whole, it seems safer to lean with the prevailing wind—to wear the stylish but uncomfortable shoes, to eat the snails, to read Charles Kingsley. Or else suffer the consequences: to be ostracized, laughed at, or stoned in the streets.

My father, a happy exception, resisted all efforts to civilize him, and why not? He had an adored uncle who deserted from the Spanish-American War, went west, and then came back to Columbus selling patent medicine with a thoroughly disreputable partner. He set up shop in a wagon at the foot of the State House steps, where he could joyfully accost his brother, my grandfather, as that very proper gentleman came down from his office in his tall silk hat—my grandfather was "in government"—and embarrass him nearly to tears. And my grandmother, who "got religion" in middle age, used to scour the streets of Columbus for bums and tramps and bring them home for Sunday dinner. With things like that in your family, you either escape into Kingsley and snails with a vengeance and never admit to Columbus, or you spend your whole life laughing. My father was of the latter persuasion. He had a hard time taking anything very seriously—except the Republican Party.

But my mother took lots of things seriously, and so it was difficult sometimes to know what to think. I solved this problem the way many of us do: I kept my mouth shut. As Hamlet would have advised, I assumed a virtue if I had it not, and what virtue I assumed had mainly to do with who I was with at the time. It was a new version of an old song: "If you're not near the people you agree with, agree with the people you're near."

Still, here I was, faced with a new husband who wanted to know why I liked a certain book. What to answer? After all, he was the expert. I had no idea what I was expected to say. Maybe I wasn't supposed to like the book. Maybe if I liked it, I was revealing ignorance or bad taste. Maybe he would stone me in the streets—metaphorically, of course. In those simpler days, pre-Betty Friedan, it didn't occur to me to say that I liked it because I liked it and so what, Buster, you want to make something of it? As I recall, I mumbled something incoherent and changed the subject. But I thought about it a lot, that simple and yet not so simple "why" and my reflexive reaction to it, which was to wonder what I was *expected* to say, rather than to wonder how best I could say what I really felt. I think in many ways it marked a turning point.

For, finally, though it's good to have an opinion, it isn't enough by itself. It isn't enough simply to say that you do or you don't like something. It's terribly important to know why, to be able to examine your own reactions and not be afraid to expound on them and, if necessary, defend them. This is true in all the parts of our lives, not just with books. But books are a good place to begin because they are readily accessible containers for someone else's ideas and style, and give the reader a good way to measure those things against his own.

Maurice Sendak has said that little children often like or dislike their picture books for reasons that may be obscure to them as well as to their parents. But surely by the time children are ready for novels like *The Water-Babies*, they are articulate enough, and enough in touch with their feelings, to make talking about their reading valuable. And surely, parents and teachers can make an effort to be liberal and accept the fact that no single book will be admired by every child in a classroom.

My mother read aloud the children's classics to my sister and me because some unknown person said they were the books we ought to hear, and it didn't occur to us to challenge that opinion, even though we were less than enthralled with some of them. They are all still in print today, including *The Water-Babies*; still on the bookstore shelf labeled CLASSICS. I know because I went and looked.

Although I realize that reading is not as popular a pastime as it used to be, and although I also realize that some children would not read at all if it weren't for classroom assignments, nevertheless it makes me uncomfortable to know that my story *Tuck Everlasting* is required reading in some classrooms. My sympathies are entirely with the children, for many will react to *Tuck* as I well might have: with a shudder. *Tuck* is not a crowd-pleaser. But it has apparently come to seem useful, particularly for classroom discussions about death, though that is not, to my mind, its central theme. If the classroom discussion could be about whether the children like it as a story, and why—or why not—that would be useful. If they could be encouraged to examine their own reactions to it as a piece of fiction, and not simply talk about whether *they* would like to live forever or not—which is a separate question—that would be useful. That would be a good first step toward developing a critical eye. If some of those who didn't like it, for their own reasons, could admit at the same time that it was nevertheless a good book—or, if some of those who did like it, for their own reasons, could admit at the same time that it was nevertheless a bad book—that would be invaluable.

But the letters I get indicate that for the most part this is not what is happening. On occasion I will get a large envelope which encloses letters from every child in a class, and all are complimentary. Obviously, the letters are part of a class assignment, an exercise, and do not involve any independent thought at all. The teacher has said, "Now we shall all write to an author," and what emerges is the same kind of good manners that we see in a Christmas thank-you note to Aunt Minnie enthusing over the lovely record album of Kate Smith's greatest hits. These poor children have just had another lesson in learning not to say that, as far as they're concerned, the emperor is walking around stark naked.

Naturally I hope that there are some children who really like my stories, and I do sometimes get letters written outside of school which are clearly sincere in their approval. And naturally I hope that, since writing letters is not to everyone's taste, there are many more children who really like my stories but don't bother to tell me about it. I myself have written only one fan letter in my life, and that was to ice skater Sonja Henie in 1938.

Actually, the most enthusiastic fan letter I ever got, though it was far from an articulate critical appraisal, was not a letter at all but a kind of graffiti, and I only heard about it secondhand. I was told by a librarian in Charlotte, North Carolina, that someone wrote in the front of a copy of *Goody Hall: This is a good book, and funny, too. Right on, Brother! No jive, funky Mama!* I suppose you could say that it is criticism of a sort, in one sense, since the writer says that the book is funny in addition to being good, not good because it's funny. But still, nice as it is, I prefer a sharply critical letter I got two years ago from a reader named Lainie Moskowitz:

Dear Miss Babbitt,

I'm a ten year old girl, who is in the fifth grade and I have just finished reading your book, The Eyes Of The Amarayllis [sic]. I'm writing this letter to inform you of some of my thoughts while reading your book. I didn't think it was very interesting because many of the parts were too confusing to understand. The book didn't give any explanation about what happened to the grandfather when he drowned. In my opinion I would [have] liked information about Jenny and Gran. I would have liked to know more about their lives and a better description of their character. I was expecting a more exciting ending. If you write

another book that you think would be more interest-
ing I'd be glad to read it.

How fine that is! If only I could have expressed my judgments as well and as fearlessly as that at the age of ten! Or even twenty! Lainie Moskowitz will never eat snails unless she truly wants to, and that makes her a rare human being: an honest one. It's good to be honest about books, good to see clearly with your critical eye. Naturally I hope that Lainie Moskowitz will not be so candid in a Christmas thank-you note, but literary criticism should have nothing to do with good manners.

We are very kind to each other in the children's book world, kind to the point that we often mislead each other, I think. At the least our reviewers search for redeeming virtues in otherwise impossible books, and at the most they are gently chiding. This does not do the writer or the reader any favors, or the poor parent who must rely on reviews or else read every one of the two thousand books published every year. There is a tendency to believe that anyone who writes for children must be good-hearted and well-intentioned, which can scarcely be proven one way or another; and even if it were true, it certainly has nothing at all to do with the quality of the product.

When I was younger and had more opinions than I do now, I more or less wanted to ban all books that didn't measure up to my opinion of what a good one was. Now I feel that it's far more important for children to make up their own minds about what they like, to be able to say why, and to learn to have confidence in their own decisions. How else will they be able, later on, to choose well among everything from brands of toothpaste to candidates for public office—choose well and independently instead of leaning like grass in the prevailing wind to all the various forms of public and private pressure?

I'm not suggesting that teachers, librarians, and parents stay out of the selection process. And I know because I have three children of my own—at least, they *used* to be children—that it's often extremely difficult to get them to read at all. But in the best of all possible worlds, the adult in charge doesn't say, "Here's a good book. The *Horn Book* says it's good, the *Washington Post* says it's good, the jacket blurb says it's good, and I say it's good. Go and read it." Neither does he or she say, "Here's a good book. Go and read it and tell me why it's good." That's a little better, but it still misses the point. Instead, the adult in charge might say, "Here's a book some people think is good. Go read it and tell me what you think." That would be lovely—to be asked by an adult what you think about something another adult has done, and to know that what you think is actually important, whether you agree with those adults or not. It implies, happily, that you are something other than a sponge.

And anyway, it's a given of human nature that we are deeply suspicious of what other people claim will be good for us. Other people always want to improve us in one way or another. To bring us up to snuff. Leafing through a recent issue of *Publishers Weekly*, I found the following phrases in reviews and advertisements: "outstanding graphic design, splendidly printed and beautifully bound"; "ingenious charm . . . instantly appealing"; "what a treat!"; "a marvelously human portrait"; "the most extraordinary book to shine under the Christmas star"; "children around the world love these books." My reaction to all this is apt to be, "Oh yeah?"

Of course, I write reviews myself, occasionally, and though I try to avoid hyperbole, still, often I do feel strongly that a book is wonderful. Or terrible. And will try to say why as clearly as possible in the space allowed. But I certainly don't expect people reading the review to say, "Oh—well—gee—is that so? Well, I guess that's right, then." I hope people will say, "Oh yeah?" and then go see for themselves.

Putting something into print, whether it's fiction or criticism or even advertising, lends it the force of authority somehow. Print is formal and assertive. It looks as if it knows what it is saying. Italics leap out; exclamation points insist; a line of type goes marching across the page like God trampling out the vintage. Learning to say "Oh yeah?" is a vitally important defense against it all. We are not, after all, going to find many advertisers, or authors, or newspaper columnists who will finish their pieces by saying, "Of course, that's only *my* opinion. You may feel that Sydney Carton was doing a far, far stupider thing than he had ever done." Or, "You may feel that our instant hollandaise sauce tastes like Elmer's Glue." Or, "You may think that killing Herman Tarnower, the diet doctor, was a dirty job but *somebody* had to do it." And since they won't say these things, but will instead go right on insisting, in print, on their own versions of the truth, we must learn early to read defensively, to read critically, to try as hard as we can to make up our own minds. To try, in other words, to take pride in thinking for ourselves.

Probably what we need to do is to demystify books, along with a number of other things. There is nothing holy, after all, about a piece of fiction except possibly to its author, and as a rule, writers who feel their works are holy are probably not very good writers, by virtue of the fact that a workmanlike detachment is at some point in the creative process absolutely essential. That's one of my more recent opinions, by the way—number eleven, if my memory serves me, which it often doesn't. Anyway, whoever said, "When in Rome, do as the Romans do," was clearly nervous about being stoned in the streets. Good manners notwithstanding, it's getting increasingly important to have a critical eye and to respect your own brain even if the expert standing next to you at the cocktail party or in front of you in the fifth-grade classroom turns hostile. As long as you know why. As John Simon, the *New York* magazine drama critic, said in a recent interview, "A critic needs to be able to explain his position."

The only reason why I don't still go around thumping on podiums about how bad most of our books for children are is that it doesn't seem much to the point anymore. And anyway, it turns out to be a very old complaint. I reread *The Water-Babies* recently to make sure it was as dreary and silly as it seemed when it was first read aloud to me forty years ago. It is. It holds up wonderfully. But toward the end, in a section where the hero is on a long journey to a place called the-Other-end-of-Nowhere, there is a paragraph that reads this way:

> *And first he went through Waste-paper-land, where all the stupid books lie in heaps, up hill and down dale, like leaves in a winter wood; and there he saw people digging . . . among them, to make worse books*

out of bad ones . . . and a very good trade they drove
thereby, especially among children.

So of course it occurred to me that it may take one to know one.

In fairness, I should tell you that Charles Kingsley wrote *The Water-Babies* in 1863, when the world was rather a different place. No doubt we should make allowances, especially as he couldn't be here to defend himself. Nevertheless, I wish we would be more careful how we bandy the term *classic* about, particularly if we catch ourselves using it to scare little children.

Once, when I was in high school, we managed to get my father to church for a midnight carol service on Christmas Eve. The church was so crowded with people putting in their annual attendance in the nick of time that, since we neglected to come half an hour early, we and a few dozen luckless others were relegated to the parish hall, where we had to listen to the service over a loudspeaker. About ten minutes into it, the loudspeaker went dead. We all sat there like good lambs in utter silence for quite a while, and then my father said in a clear voice, "This church doesn't need a minister. What this church needs is a good electrician."

The effect of this remark was exactly like that of the child's remark in the story of the emperor's clothes. It appeared that everyone in the parish house agreed. And it appeared that everyone was grateful to my father for bringing the subject up. There were general exclamations of relief, and then we all wished each other a merry Christmas and went home to bed. If it had not been for my father's fearlessly voicing an opinion, we might have sat there trying not to look at each other for hours and hours, afraid of being stoned.

The years ahead are going to be full of increasingly difficult problems, all of which will require courage and a good critical eye in the solving. My opinion number twelve is that if we want a peaceful old age, we'd better start now training our children to say what they think. I would like to suggest that wherever there are two or three gathered together, they be sat down to listen to that certified classic *The Water-Babies*, and then be encouraged to express themselves. It's as good a place as any to begin, and it just might make a difference.

Publicity photograph for Farrar, Straus and Giroux by Thomas
Victor, 1983

" *I remember my childhood vividly—what it felt like, what I thought about,
what I did and said as opposed to what other children did and said.*

"

The Way We Were—and Weren't

(1985)

My home state, Ohio, has always been a hard state to figure. More presidents were born there than in any other state in the union except Virginia, but none, with the possible exception of Taft, were memorable. Two were even assassinated, which makes you wonder. I live in Rhode Island now, and Rhode Island has the same sort of reputation that Ohio has: a place you hurry through on your way to somewhere else. I'm not going somewhere else. At least I hope not. I like Rhode Island. My roots go deep in Ohio, though. My ancestors were there long before it was Ohio, and none of them hurried on to somewhere else. In this they may have shown a serious lack of imagination.

But I left Ohio when I got married in 1954 and have lived in Connecticut, Tennessee, Washington, DC, central New York State, Massachusetts, New York City, and now Rhode Island in the forty years since. Sometimes I think all that moving has been bad for me, and sometimes I don't. Sometimes I don't because, you see, my family moved around a lot in Ohio, too, long before I got married, and so I went to a lot of very different kinds of schools, and met a lot of very different kinds of children.

I remember my childhood vividly—what it felt like, what I thought about, what I did and said as opposed to what other children did and said. My views on the variety of types of children were and are the same as my views now on the variety of types of adults. So it always comes as a shock to me to hear people talk about "the child." I'm never sure what child they mean.

I have a sister who is two years older than I am, and we were never very much alike. There's a truly distressing snapshot of the two of us at ages seven and nine, sitting on a park bench. We are dressed alike, but that's where the likeness stops, because she was overweight and I was emaciated. The dresses we're wearing have puffed sleeves, and my arms hang as loose in those sleeves as the clappers in a pair of bells, while my sister's cuffs are like tourniquets. A sorry sight indeed. We were different in more important ways, too. She was an excellent student, while I was what teachers now tactfully refer to as an underachiever. She was gregarious and I was pretty much of a hermit. If anyone had tried to define us as "the child," the confusion would have been substantial.

People say to me occasionally, "Do you have 'the child' in

mind when you write?" What child? Myself? My sister? Or possibly Tempy Pitts? Tempy Pitts—full name Temperance Pitts—has assumed for me by now something of the status of a folk hero. She was in my sister's class and she was a member of one of those families from West Virginia and Kentucky who, in those days, came across the Ohio River, when summer was over, to find work in the southern Ohio factories. Our town was the home of Armco Steel and attracted great numbers of these families—known locally as "poor white trash"—who would dutifully enroll their children in the schools and then, at the end of the school year, go home again back across the river and live all summer on what they'd earned. This particular fall, my sister's third-grade teacher was taking her students through the annual September ritual of telling what they'd done during the vacation. When it was Tempy's turn, the teacher said, "Now, Tempy, tell us about your summer." And Tempy stood up and said, "Aw, ah jus' run up 'n' down a mountain 'n' eat a piece of bread."

So do I have Tempy Pitts in mind when I write? Of course. Tempy is always in my mind, I'm happy to say. I am less happy to say that Norma Cox is also always in my mind. Norma Cox was in *my* class. She was little and even thinner than I was, and her clothes were even thinner than that, and we all avoided her. I was once kind to Norma Cox for half an hour at recess and will never forget the surprise and gratitude on her pinched little face. I then, with the supreme cruelty of childhood, ignored her ever after, feeling that I had done my duty and could face my Sunday school teacher with a clear conscience.

So—yes, I have Norma Cox in mind, but also Janie Dorner.

Janie Dorner was blond and beautiful, with shiny straight hair, and sweaters that matched her socks, and she was always smiling, in spite of the fact that *her* older sister, equally beautiful, was an epileptic who sometimes had seizures in school.

There was Beth McKinnon, who passed through my second grade only briefly. She was, as I recall, a certified genius who could draw like Leonardo da Vinci when she was only seven, and was soon placed in some special school where she could blossom. Before she came, I was the best artist in my class. I was the one who got to draw the princess for our frieze of the story about the princess on the glass mountain. Beth put my nose out of joint and I was very glad when she left.

Do I write for Beth McKinnon? Certainly not. Let her write her own stories.

There was June Green, who had to miss a chunk of third grade when one of her many siblings got bitten by a mad dog and the whole family had to get dreadful, debilitating hydrophobia shots that took weeks to recover from. June was shy and pale and earnest. But Jane Rettig was ruddy and assertive, even in grammar school, and she gave great birthday parties. There was Marsha Klein, who spent her summers in Minnesota and expected everyone to be impressed by the fact. I guess I was impressed—I've remembered those vacations for more than fifty years. And then there was Sudie Riley, who was spoiled and had mountains of toys, and tended to be mean to her cat.

As for boys, I fell in love in the first grade with Dwight Neill and was faithful to him until we moved away in the middle of sixth grade. My mother, driving by the school once when we were out for recess in second grade, saw me corner Dwight among the bicycle racks and kiss him. He was very handsome, and I didn't and don't apologize.

And there was, ever and always, my sister, my hero, with her stunningly large vocabulary and her tree house where she read *Little Women* and *Oliver Twist* and sobbed up there among the catalpa pods while I, down below, in answer to some obscure diabolical urge, occasionally strung up a noose or two and lynched my dolls, a ritual which seems to have worried no one.

So, tell me, who is "the child" we hear so much about? The children I remember had precious little in common. Well, I'll tell you who "the child" is. "The child" is a construction put together by adults, that's who. "The child," once out of diapers, does not cry. "The child" is beautiful and honest and is never without a Kleenex. "The child" watches some television, but accepts parental guidance cheerfully, and would rather read, anyway. "The child" is clean all the time except when being picturesquely dirty. "The child" is never sick except for measles, mumps, and chicken pox, which are passed through with forbearance, with dispatch, and without scratching. "The child" is not afraid of the dark or of swimming or dogs or Great-Aunt Esther's mustache. "The child" has better manners than Amy Vanderbilt. "The child" will qualify for Harvard without ever being a bookworm or a grind. "The child," in short, will go out into the world and stun everyone, especially jealous relatives, with his or her splendid genetic makeup and obviously superior parenting, a combination of nature and nurture impossible to improve on, thereby insuring lasting self-satisfaction for "the parent."

"The child," then, is as utterly different from anyone we know personally as are "children." "Children," once you get past our national concept of them as "the future," are not necessarily desirable or attractive on a day-to-day basis. And they are certainly not important except insofar as they will someday be adults. Childhood is something to be got through as quickly as possible so you can get to the good stuff that comes with maturity, and one part of the good stuff is evidently the privilege of looking back and being sentimental about childhood. This means, of course, that one's own childhood was either sweet beyond the dreams of paradise, or difficult beyond the novels of Charles Dickens. So maybe it would be more accurate to say that one's own self as a child was important, but children in general are not. In the eyes of the world they're not, anyway. If they were, we would pay our elementary-school teachers a living wage.

The problem appears to be that children are not a power group. They don't have any money. If they had money, we'd probably let them vote. But they don't. Not enough, anyway. They also don't have any experience—that golden quality, so hard-won, that makes it possible for us adults to conduct our lives without any mistakes in judgment, without any problems, without noise or social disruption or unreasonable behavior of any kind. Children are also unfinished as to education. They have not yet read Proust, like us, and they don't understand the words all the singers are singing when they go to the opera, and they don't read the *New York Times* front to back every day the way we do. And— they don't know how to spell *rhinoceros*. We, of course, all know how to spell *rhinoceros*. The ability to spell *rhinoceros* is one of the hallmarks of an educated person, and children have yet to come to it.

It is for these reasons that people who write children's books are suspect. The world looks at us in a puzzled way and wonders, "Why devote your life to writing for a group that has no money, no experience, and can't spell *rhinoceros?* Such writing can't be serious." And it isn't just us writers. My husband once worked for Memorial Sloan Kettering Cancer Center in New York City, and one time at a party I talked to the chief of pediatric services. He told me gloomily that pediatric services are classed among other medical services just as children's books are classed with books for other ages. So, whatever it is, if it has to do with children, it's got no clout.

Some of my colleagues are very defensive about their work. Many say sniffily that they *don't* write for children—they write to please themselves. Beatrix Potter even said it. But I say horsefeathers. All writers hope to please themselves by what they write; but it seems to me that it's possible to please oneself at the same time as one is writing for, and hoping to please, children. Why not? Why should those two things be mutually exclusive?

I want it understood, by the way, that when I use the term *children*, I do not mean it to include teenagers. Teenagers are something else again. One does not call them children in their presence and expect to be applauded, and in fact, they aren't children, technically, because they aren't powerless. It's doubtful that they have much experience, and my guess is that few of them can spell *rhinoceros*, but the thing is, they've got money. So they have the most telling kind of importance. I read somewhere recently that the big spender now for movies is a fourteen-year-old boy. Hollywood producers are taking this into account. And that's clout.

Writers of books for teenagers are higher up the prestige scale than writers of books for the prepube group. This is because the public is afraid of teenagers, and imagines that people who write books for them have some inside track on understanding them. I imagine this, myself. My picture of the situation is that during the teenage years, people are far more alike than they were as children, and far more alike than they will be as adults. This picture makes of life a sort of hourglass with the top part labeled CHILDHOOD, the squeezed-in neck part labeled TEEN-AGERS, and the bottom labeled ADULTHOOD.

Or let me put that another way. Childhood is South America (even though it's at the top) in all its warm and infinite variety from Rio to the Andes. Adulthood is North America (even though it's at the bottom) with its cold Canadian fronts and all that open land demanding to be dug up and built on. And the teenage years are the Panama Canal: hot and volatile, with everyone in battle fatigues, looking utterly inscrutable.

Well, I am probably wrong. But I was a teenager in that pointless and arid period between Frank Sinatra and Elvis Presley, and so have grown up uninitiated. I collected Mario Lanza records. When I went away to college and was feeling lonely and homesick, I'd just slip up to my room and put on a 45 recording of Lanza singing "Be My Love." A person who is turned on by "Be My Love" is not going to find common coin with the Rolling Stones.

So, anyway, teenagers are not children, and I don't write for them. This has caused no outcry in the high schools, so it's all right. My books are for children: specifically, I guess, for the last best year of childhood, the fifth grade. And I resent fifth graders being lumped together into some great, unformed ball of clay called "the child."

There are a lot of special things about fifth grade. Or, at least, there were a lot of special things about my fifth grade. I didn't know I didn't have any clout, you see. I didn't realize the full importance of money, and I was never asked to spell *rhinoceros*. There was a war on—we were all very much aware of *that*—but I didn't read the newspapers front to back to keep up on its progress. And although I was in love with Dwight Neill, it was as innocent a love in fifth grade as in any fairy tale. It became a little less innocent in sixth grade, with the advent of games like post office and spin the bottle, but we moved away before any harm was done.

The thing is, I don't want to hear about "the child," that mythical monster we are all supposed to have in mind when we write. I have in mind only myself and all my fifth-grade classmates, from Marcia Ellison, my jolly best friend, to Larry Jones, who died of leukemia, to Donald Crawley, the class jock, to Georgie Bach, who loved me, to Ruth Upton, who didn't. We were not "the child"—we were people. Separate, distinct, with different dreams and different sorrows.

If we were the future then, now, grown up, we are in large part the past. But all of us at any given moment are the present, and that is what matters. Our childhoods, our adulthoods, our old age, are only a long series of nows, a continuing present where we are always people first and foremost, separate and distinct, regardless of our age. It's a good thing for all of us to remember: parents, teachers, writers, all of us who work with and for children, all of us who were once children ourselves. And that really is all of us.

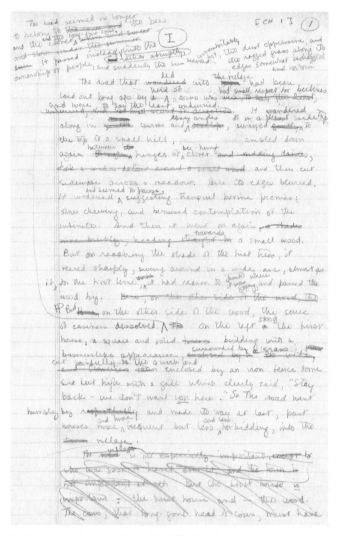

Early manuscript page from *Tuck Everlasting*

> *For our fiction, we must construct a life that is not average, not 'true to life.' We must construct a plot, and figure out again and again something that can happen, something that will carry conflicts and demons to our child heroes, since they have none ready-made inside their heads.*

Something Has to Happen

(*1985*)

I t has occurred to me recently that there is a difference between juvenile and adult fiction which is so obvious that it has
escaped at least *my* attention, though I and all of us who write for
children have always had to deal with it: Child heroes, like their
flesh-and-blood counterparts, being powerless, innocent, and
mainly unformed, are acted upon rather than acting. That seems
simple, and yet it profoundly affects the construction of a story
and defines a fundamental variance between the two literatures.

Since the child hero is acted upon, there has to be a plot to a
children's story. Without exterior action there can be no story at
all. Interior action—that is, the workings of a character's thoughts,

personality, and the accumulated experience of his own life and that of the people around him—is rare in children's books. Children, and by association child heroes, haven't been around long enough; they are not experienced enough to be much guided by reflection, and have very little control over their own lives. Things must, therefore, happen *to* them, things from which we hope they will learn. And things happening is simply another term for the unfolding of a plot.

Things used to have to happen in adult fiction, too, but not anymore. Short stories in the *New Yorker*, for instance, are mostly devoid of events. They have no discernible plots. The idea of things happening is so unusual nowadays in adult fiction that Joseph Heller could call his long-awaited second novel *Something Happened* and keep us turning the pages to find out what in the world it would turn out to be. I suppose you could say that modern adult fiction accurately reflects modern adult life, at least here in safe and insulated America. Nothing much does happen to most of us, after all—nothing you could call an adventure—unless we make it happen, which fact is apt to come as a distinct surprise.

Perhaps this is why adventure novels, and adventure movies like *Raiders of the Lost Ark*, seem to critics to be fare only for the unsophisticated—escape fare which bears no relationship to reality. But whether this is true or not, there is a difference even between adult adventure novels and movies, and those intended for children. Even though the action in both is all exterior, the heroes are different: The older ones act; the younger are acted upon.

You could probably make the claim, without too much fear

of contradiction, that all stories for children are adventure stories, if by that you mean stories in which the action is exterior. This may be too broad an interpretation of the term *adventure*, and yet it would be difficult to find a children's novel in which the child hero does not have an adventure of some sort, an adventure on which the plot hangs and from which the child hero will learn the necessary lesson. For there must be a lesson, though that is a more disagreeable way of putting it than to say that the hero must change somehow and thereby grow. Child heroes will always change somehow, even though they are almost always the tools of the action rather than its initiator.

The rare child hero who does initiate action must do it in secrecy, and always in fear of being discovered by an adult. There is exhilaration in the secrecy, perhaps, but it is also inhibiting and makes these heroes furtive little people, while the adults around them come off as remarkably obtuse and credulous. The children in the movie *E.T.* keep their alien hidden till the very end. They can do nothing overt. They know, like Mary and Colin in *The Secret Garden*, that they will not be allowed to act if their project is known.

It would seem that we are not saying anything very healthy about honesty and authority in stories like these, but they do reflect the fact that if, in real life, children are to act, independently and imaginatively, if they are to make things happen, they must, as in their fiction, be deceitful. Deceitful or forthright, however, the nature of the action remains the same: It is all exterior.

What does that really mean? To grasp the difference, you have to think about the difference between the two heroes. A child hero is, almost without exception and in spite of small aberrations, going to be likeable, rational, bright, and attractive. Remember, we are talking here about children's novels, not teenage novels. Action in teenage novels more often than not revolves around a young hero's learning how to be likeable, rational, bright, and attractive. Teenage novels, whatever else they may entail, are concerned at bottom with rejection and acceptance, and their action falls somewhere between the interior and the exterior. But never mind that; the child hero and the adult hero are what concern us here.

Since child heroes are, as I have suggested, normally likeable, rational, bright, and attractive, their character is not in itself going to bring about conflict. The conflict must come from the outside—must be visited on them by forces that are big, in size and scope, and powerful. Evil and good are clearly differentiated, and these heroes will respond in ways that are dictated by their innocence, their sense of justice, their love. They have a largeness and simplicity of soul—a nobility, if you will—that ensures their successful coping. The end of their adventures will be happy. They will have learned something, they will have grown and changed, and they will be the better for it.

Modern adult heroes are something quite different. When their stories begin, they will already have been scarred by at least two decades of living. The twig has been bent one way or another before chapter 1, unless there is some reason for narrating the process of bending, and the resultant tree is a little crooked. As their stories unfold, they are, typically, themselves the engineers of the action, at the mercy of their own preconceptions and their uncertain sense of self. They will face choices, try to make decisions, and compromise again and again because right and wrong are blurred for them, and run together. The conflicts are inside their own heads, and whatever resolutions there may be are determined by the shape of their own personalities. Typically, these days, they are unheroic. Typically, these days, they neither win nor lose but end, as they began, in a sort of limbo. There are, of course, exterior events; often the heroes have brought these about, themselves, through some act of recklessness or vanity. But the events are not there to move a plot along; they are there to demonstrate the heroes' pain and fallibility. Their thoughts are often the only action there is—interior, personal, narrow in scope, and, we must admit, true to life. The goal for these heroes is simply to learn to coexist with their personal demons.

Do children not have interior conflicts and personal demons? Of course they do. And heaven knows they often act out of recklessness and vanity. But from an adult perspective the scale is utterly different; the stakes are utterly different; the conflicts and demons are demonstrably controllable. All that is required for inner peace, it would seem, is obedience, with all the rewards that obedience can bring. It's hard to build a story around that, if you want to write something heftier than *Peter Rabbit*. Few of us can make anything memorable out of the small commonplaces in the life of an average child, Beverly Cleary being a notable and laudable exception.

And so, for our fiction, we must construct a life that is not average, not "true to life." We must construct a plot, and figure out again and again something that can happen, something that will carry conflicts and demons to our child heroes, since they have none ready-made inside their heads. Their battles will be overt, outside their heads, and of course they will win. Their stories, fantasy or "real," are every adventure story—always old, always new, always predictable and satisfying.

It's hard to say how long any one of us can continue to find fresh ways to tell what is essentially the same tale. This is probably the most difficult problem for writers of adventure stories, no matter who the audience and regardless of the medium. Increasingly we rely on special effects applied to reworkings of old settings, dressing the demons in costumes that grow more and more outlandish—or more and more subtle. But fresh ways are out there, or in there, somewhere, and the tantalizing challenge of finding them keeps us going—that and the fact that the need to keep telling the story is very great even if, as the critics suggest, it does not reflect reality. If it does not, then the fault lies with reality, not with our stories. Problems ought to have solutions; heroism ought to be possible. In the worlds we work so hard to create, they do and it is, and if we must cope along the way with the strictures of the form, so be it.

The author (left) with her sister, Diane, and
Big Mike, 1935

" *I have shared my life continuously with dogs . . . And yet I will confess that
when I think about them, they don't quite have the faces of dogs, somehow.
Their faces, in my mental pictures of them, are rather blurred and
indistinct, but decidedly more human than canine . . . Giving human speech
to nonhuman life is one of the most endearing things we do in our fantasies.* "

The Roots—and Branches— of Fantasy

(1986)

The thing to remember about fantasy, it seems to me, is that it's deeply rooted in reality. It didn't start out in story form. It's older than that. The fantasies came first; then the stories came along to embody them. When you're writing a fantasy story, you'd better understand that and keep it at the front of your mind, or the story won't work. For fantasy is primarily a symbolic language for dealing with three very real and fundamental human attributes: We fear, we hope, and, because life can be very dull sometimes, we need to be diverted. Of course, these three categories have a way of blurring into each other at the edges. Superstition, for instance, lies between fear and hope, and overlaps both. But in general, you can cover most of the territory by sticking to the big three.

Fear fantasies can be defined as what we don't want to believe. Hope fantasies are what we do want to believe. And diversion fantasies are what we half believe because they make life more interesting.

Fear first. Not surprisingly, it divides itself into its own categories. There is, for instance, the fear that comes from misinterpreting the facts. Let's say you are waked in the middle of the night by a thumping noise. Immediately your imagination supplies possible explanations. The furnace is getting ready to blow up. Someone has broken into the house and is looking for your grandmother's silver. Someone has broken into the house and is looking for *you*. Someone is on the roof, and it isn't Santa Claus because it isn't December twenty-fourth. Why would someone be on the roof? There is no healthy answer, so the only answers your imagination can come up with are all unhealthy. In my most recent encounter with night thumps, investigation the following day revealed that our neighbor in the other half of our converted carriage house was banging on his ceiling with a broom handle in an effort to dislodge a bunch of pigeons who were holding a convention on the roof over his bedroom. The truth is very often a letdown.

Other kinds of fantasies arising from misinterpretation of the facts might include discovering a bump on your foot which leads you to conclude that you have somehow contracted jungle rot and have only hours to live. Subsequently you find out that the bump is a bunion. Jungle rot would have been far more romantic.

In the picture-book story *Bedtime for Frances*, Frances sees an ominous shape in the corner of her room at night. She thinks it is a monster, but it turns out to be her bathrobe draped over a chair. A relief, and yet—somehow also a disappointment. And then, of course, there's the story of Chicken Little, she on whom the sky fell.

These are modern misinterpretations, but because we have all experienced them, it ought to be easy to understand our caveman ancestors' fear of thunder, for instance, and the colorful explanations their own imaginations provided.

A second type of fear fantasy is caused by fear of the unknown. First and foremost here is fear of death. What fun we've had down the centuries personifying death in stories! It's usually a male figure: the Grim Reaper with his scythe, or a hooded wraith with skeletal limbs like Scrooge's Ghost of Christmas Yet to Come. It is closely tied to Satan on the one hand, like Melville's white whale, and to natural but chilling human remains on the other, like the skull and crossbones on a pirate flag or a bottle of poison. Sometimes, certainly, it is represented as some kind of benevolent angelic force, as in the death of Beth March in *Little Women*, or that of little Paul Dombey in Dickens's *Dombey and Son*. But these are hope fantasies, not fear fantasies, though Dickens can turn it all around in the same novel and bring it crashing down on his villain in the form of an onrushing train, where it is very much a fear fantasy.

Other fears of the unknown might be the lifelong recurring question as to whether or not there is something unnamed and indescribable under the bed. Or down in a corner of the cellar. Something that moves fast and has unfathomable purposes, none of them good. We have all raced up many a flight of cellar stairs in our day. Or night. And we have kept our hands on top of the bed.

A subtype of this fear of the unknown is fear of strangers. The unidentified voice on the telephone. The ringing of the doorbell when we're in the house alone. The shadowy figure on the sidewalk after dark. I just used, above, the word *unnamed*, and that's an important element if you want a character or a substance or an object to suggest evil. A student of mine once wrote a story in which two girls were investigating a pair of witches. At first she had the witches dropping the customary wing of bat and eye of newt into a cauldron, but between us we decided it would be far more effective if they dropped in a heavy, unnamed something wrapped in newspaper. In my story *Tuck Everlasting*, the man in the yellow suit had a name in an early draft. Later I took it out. Named, he was somehow accessible, and therefore diminished. Unnamed, he was a stranger and suggestive, therefore, of fear and evil.

Beyond death and the unknown, there is also the fear of losing control of normalcy, as the children do in Chris Van Allsburg's *Jumanji*. This can mean losing what we like to imagine is the control we have over our natural environment, control which is erased in earthquakes, floods, plagues, and hurricanes. Or it can mean losing control of ourselves—our bodies or our minds. Robert Cormier is a master at stories where things go haywire and people lose control. Edgar Allan Poe was no slouch at it, either. And the old TV series *The Twilight Zone* embodied it perfectly.

Whatever type of fear it is, in whatever type of story, the chills the storyteller brings to the story are enriched by what our own fantasies, with their ancient roots, provide as we listen or read. And yet, by means of our fantasies, we not only flesh out and personalize the fear, but also, most of the time, we provide the means for coping with it. So fantasy stories based on fears are in the end therapeutic. They allow us to name the unnameable and face the unfaceable. They allow us to become the hero.

A brief parenthesis here about superstition. Superstitions define punishments for various crimes, but they also provide methods for prevention. If you don't walk under the ladder, if you don't break the mirror, you'll be all right. However, there are other superstitions, having to do with random occurrences, that have no prevention spelled out. One I came across recently is that it's a sure sign you're going to be in trouble if your cow moos three times in your face. Presumably, however, if you're aware of this downside to mooing, you can simply arrange not to stand face-to-face with your cow.

Hope fantasies are just as universal as those dealing with fear. A lot of our favorite fairy tales are hope fantasies, and most of the time they have to do with ego satisfactions of one kind or another. But we are full enough of these without having to resort to reading the Brothers Grimm to find them. They are with us every day.

Our view of our personal appearance makes a good example. Everyone who sees us knows what we look like. But we don't. Not really. We are full of fantasies about ourselves. What else can explain the terrible shock of catching a glimpse of ourselves unexpectedly in a mirror? "Who," we wonder, "is that tacky-looking woman?" And then we realize it's us we're looking at, and the heart drops into the shoes. But ego is a wonderfully elastic thing.

A few minutes later it has bounded back, and we're ready for the next shock.

The wish to feel better about ourselves seems to be responsible for most of the fantasies we have about ourselves. My mother believed that if a certain courthouse in Maryland hadn't burned down, she'd have been able to prove she was a descendant of Martha Washington. My father believed to the end of his days that his ship would come in, a belief that made me wonder, when I was very small, how that ship was going to make its way down our street in southern Ohio.

The belief that we are, or soon will be, beautiful, aristocratic, rich—surely these are three of the most common themes in all hope fantasies, perhaps in all fiction. They are the three usual routes to love and power. They imply nobility, and nobility implies virtue, which in turn implies heavenly reward. Cinderella is able to marry into money and an aristocratic heritage because she is beautiful, which includes having small feet. The feet alone would let most of us out. But we are somehow able to go right on identifying with her anyway.

Romance novels capitalize on these hope fantasies, and therefore prosper. So does the world of advertising. But we believe because we want to believe, not because of Madison Avenue coercion. It's pleasant to believe that if we use Estée Lauder's vanishing cream, we will look like Elizabeth Taylor. Or if we use Charles Atlas's muscle-building machines, no one will ever kick sand in our faces again.

Some hope fantasies, sponsored by a great variety of institutions, offer easy answers to difficult problems. For instance, if we read the *New York Times* every day, the act will have a positive effect on the arms race. If we quit smoking, we will live forever. If we can get our children to stop watching TV, they'll be accepted at Harvard. And if our children get into Harvard, they will be forever after happy and successful. And rich.

Ah, money! How many of our hope fantasies revolve around money. My mother, otherwise a very intelligent and perceptive person, had this idea that all rich people are good—a notion somehow connected with the belief that money is a reward for noble behavior, as in the novels of Horatio Alger. And, incidentally, as in many children's stories, especially fairy tales. The hero or heroine begins poor and lowly, like Ali Baba, and because of virtuous, clever behavior, he or she ends up with a large bank account.

But sometimes it isn't a virtuous or clever act that turns things around. Sometimes the turning is due simply to the intervention of good luck in the shape of a fairy godmother. The fairy godmother takes many forms in our fantasies of hope. She can be a distant relative we didn't even know we had, who will die and leave us ten thousand shares of IBM stock. She can be a plastic surgeon who will turn back the clock thirty years with nothing but a needle and thread. She can be as formless as the state lottery or as specific as the only eight-legged fairy godmother in all of literature, E. B. White's Charlotte.

There are psychiatrists who say that the kind of wishful thinking represented in fantasies of hope is very bad for us, that it blocks out reality and keeps us from facing the truth. The Bible says flat out that the truth shall make you free. But I don't always go along with that, and neither did T. S. Eliot, for he said in *Murder in the Cathedral* that "Human kind cannot bear very much reality." And it seems a peculiarly contradictory thing for the Bible to say in one place that truth is liberating when in another place it puts hope on a level with faith and charity as something devoutly to be pursued. For hope and truth don't always go together. Many truths do not set us free. They can often pave the way to resignation and despair. But hope can often keep us going. *The Little Engine That Could* is in many ways a monotonous and irritating story, but it demonstrates the point admirably.

There is one other category to touch on, and that is fantasies of diversion. These don't try to demonstrate anything much; they merely entertain us. And we are very, very fond of them. Students of television advertising—as who of us is not?—will know what I mean. There have been a lot of memorable little fantasy plays acted out in the minutes devoted to ads. Who can forget the naval officer in that rowboat in the toilet tank? Or the talking margarine? Or the enchanting golden retriever puppy with his pacifier on a blue ribbon around his neck? There is charm even in the Fruit of the Loom guys and the Keebler elves. These fantasies were not made for children. They were made for us. They are trivialities, to be sure. Our lives are not improved by them in any measurable way. But they have tremendous appeal. Their silliness makes us laugh, and we need laughter. And, like fantasies of fear and hope, they are rooted in reality, if only in the reality of the frequent silliness of our own thoughts.

I have shared my life continuously with dogs. One dog after another, and sometimes two or three at a time. I have cleaned up after them; sat up with them through thunderstorms; vacuumed up their hairs; pursued their fleas with collars, powders, sprays, and exterminators; spent time and money on endless veterinarians for shots, X-rays, pills, and bandages. I have even driven our current dog, Rosie, long miles to visit two separate veterinary gastroenterologists on the advice of two separate regular vets who couldn't get to the bottom, so to speak, of her terrible intestinal problems.

These four-legged creatures have been indisputably *dogs*. And yet I will confess that when I think about them, they don't quite have the faces of dogs, somehow. Their faces, in my mental pictures of them, are rather blurred and indistinct, but decidedly more human than canine. I suspect that I am not alone in this. In fact, I know I am not alone. So do the dog-food people. So of course we are entranced by dogs who talk in television commercials, or by rabbits who talk in books as small and simple as Beatrix Potter's or as long and complex as *Watership Down*. Giving human speech to nonhuman life is one of the most endearing things we do in our fantasies of diversion, though I should point out that we do it in our fear and hope fantasies, too. Perhaps we do it because we are lonely. I don't know. I do know that we sometimes do it to point out things that would seem too harsh or preachy if our characters were human beings. But most of the time we do it simply because it gives us pleasure.

There is another kind of fantasy of diversion that has been around longer than the pyramids, and this kind involves creatures we wish were there but aren't. Generation after generation, we pass along the Tooth Fairy and Santa Claus, more than willing to risk the indignation of our children when they find out it's all a tissue of lies. But then they grow up and join us in our wistful longing for proof that there really is a Loch Ness monster, an

Abominable Snowman, a Bigfoot. Expensive expeditions go out again and again to look for these creatures and they never find anything. But no expedition is ever the once-and-for-all final expedition. Like psychosomatics going from doctor to doctor in search of confirmation that they really are sick, we are never satisfied with the diagnosis that there is nothing there. And why should we be? Life is infinitely more interesting when we can believe in the possibility of something wonderful hidden just over the next hill, to be discovered at last by just one more expensive expedition. For, every once in a while, a tenacious and fantasy-laden person does find something wonderful. With nothing more to go on than that well-known myth Homer's *Iliad*, Heinrich Schliemann went out and dug up Troy.

All fantasy is rooted somewhere very deep in reality. It is the voice of our reachings-out for explanations of the riddles of our lives and for enrichment of their texture. All can be set forth in stories told in many different ways: in dream stories like *Alice in Wonderland*, in stories where the fantasy world exists across some kind of threshold as with Oz and Narnia, in stories where some single element of fantasy appears in the hard, real world as with *Charlotte's Web*, or in stories where a rich fantasy world coexists on the same plane with reality, as Shakespeare presented it in such plays as *The Tempest* and *A Midsummer Night's Dream*.

And little by little some fantasies come true. My mother had an expression she used to demonstrate impossibility: She would say, "Why, I could no more do that than fly to the moon!" I find myself saying the same thing sometimes before I remember it's no longer an impossibility. In my favorite childhood version of "Beauty and the Beast," Beauty found, in a room in the

Beast's palace, a picture that could move and talk—and now we have television. A real gorilla has a real kitten for a pet, and has his picture taken while he cuddles it. There is a kind of photography now that can create a three-dimensional image that isn't really there at all.

In these terrible days of uncertainty, and fear not just for our own individual lives but for the life of our lovely, lonely planet, we need our fantasies more than ever, especially our fantasies of hope. I wish the adult world could recognize that need, and stop insisting that such things are only for children. For these fantasies are not something to retreat into, not sand in which we can bury our heads. They are the voices of our innermost cravings for pleasure and beauty and peace. Oh, Charlotte, how lovely if you could come back and spin a miraculous web of words at the next summit meeting! If our leaders won't listen to us, surely they are human, with hope fantasies of their own, and maybe they would listen to you.

Babbitt's illustration for the poem "Library," from
Small Poems Again (1986) by Valerie Worth

" *It is our job to do the very best we can to stimulate as much love of reading
as we can.* "

Easy Does It

(1986)

Will things be golden in the future? When you get to be my age, it's far more common to believe that things were only golden in the past. You mostly have to be the age of Little Orphan Annie, in her Broadway show, in order to belt out a song about how you love tomorrow. For people over forty, it's more appropriate to sing about memories, like the old cat in that other Broadway show.

I suppose the reasons for this are not very complicated. But they go beyond the fact that the young have more tomorrows than yesterdays, while the over-forty group probably has it the other way around. A lot of it has also to do with an ongoing and all-too-human dissatisfaction with the present: a conviction that the world is going to hell in a handbasket. People of all eras have always believed the world was going to hell in a handbasket and that things were better at some other time, usually before. Before the appearance of the waltz, for instance, which marked the onset of moral decay. Or, if not the waltz, then before automobiles, or before the war (any war), before movies, before television.

It's easy to imagine a couple of elderly cavemen sitting around complaining about the invention of the wheel. Oog might say, "Well, there goes honest labor and life lived at a reasonable pace." And Mog might reply, "You're right. Why, when I was a boy, I had to lug the mammoth meat ten miles home on my back. It wasn't easy, but it built character."

We don't know exactly how fire was discovered, but a lot of people must have believed it signaled the end of the world, until Oog's wife accidentally dropped a mammoth joint on a pile of hot coals, which was the first glorious step toward boil-in-a-bag turkey tetrazzini.

It's hard to believe anyone could have thought things were better before fire. But look at it this way: Oog's wife may have been barefoot and pregnant a lot, but before fire, she certainly didn't have to spend any time in the kitchen.

The point is that change has always seemed to come in sudden great leaps instead of gradually, depriving people over thirty, say, of the necessary time to prepare their minds and their lives. Like Oog and Mog, adults sometimes don't know what to make of it all, and that creates crankiness and resistance. I say people over thirty because it's been amply demonstrated that before that time, we are more flexible. We haven't got set in our ways yet, and we're too inexperienced to anticipate difficulties. Look at Rubik's Cube. Average kids could solve it in a few carefree, intuitive twists. But their average elders looked at it and said to themselves, "This looks hard! Gee—six colors!" And proceeded to try to apply reason to it, thereby making any intuitive solution impossible.

I remember watching on TV the first space-rocket liftoff with tears in my eyes, it was so beautiful and astonishing. But my children, then three, five, and seven, were utterly blasé. They were so new themselves that they couldn't really grasp other newnesses—if there is such a word. What did they care that, in the good old days, people had been wont to say, when confronted with a difficulty, "Might as well try to fly to the moon"?

In the good old days when I was a child, there seemed to be a lot more room in houses. And I don't especially remember anyone being annoyed about too few electrical outlets. But now the average house, mostly built in the thirties or forties, is jammed with electric and electronic gadgets and too many twisting extension cords, making it look rather like a combination of Dr. Frankenstein's laboratory and a snake pit. In my kitchen, you have to unplug either the dustbuster or the humidifier before you can plug in the toaster. The dustbuster has to stay plugged in all the time because, you see, it's cordless. The only time it's not plugged in is when you're using it. When you really stop to think about that, you want to run screaming into the wilderness, except there's no wilderness left to run screaming into. And as for the humidifier, it has to run all the time from September to May because the modern furnace is so efficient that it dries out everything from furniture glue to the dog's water dish in a mere twinkling. The toaster, however, is more humble. Nothing newfangled about the toaster. It burns bread just as nicely as the toasters of my childhood.

Everywhere the humble hunches up next to the new. We live in half of a carriage house that was built around 1880, and has recently been gutted, the interior rebuilt to make it very contemporary. But the original brick walls were kept un-plastered-over, inside and out, and though they let in winter winds as generously as a screen door, they're very nice and humble to look at. However, against one of them, the television set with its great gray empty face sits on a sort of rolling table. On top of the television set is a box for controls of the cable system, a box that looks like a squashed Darth Vader helmet. And on a shelf below is the sleek new VCR. Behind it all, wires and switches hang down, reach out, and tangle up, with their plugs pressed to the outlet like hungry mouths.

Well, we're used to all this proliferation of electric things. And our gadgets do make our lives easier and more pleasant; no point denying that. Ease and pleasure are what it's always been about, from the wheel all the way up to the digital watch. No one has ever invented something in order to make life more difficult. At least, not on purpose.

So—what, after all, was so good about the good old days? I can remember my mother doing laundry in the 1930s, standing for long periods in the basement on cold concrete while she fed our sopping clothes through a wringer she had to turn by hand. And then she had to hang everything outside on a line. It took her all day. And all of another day to iron everything. All I have to do—well, you know how easy it is, and I never iron. I own an iron, but it's the least-used thing in the house.

Does hard work really build character? Oog and Mog thought so. Are things that are easy and pleasant bad for us? Our Puritan forebears thought so. I don't have an opinion on it. One man's easy is another man's hard, is what I think. Most progress has two sides to it, some good, some bad, and that's true for just about everything.

There are a lot of concerns about today's education, but it seems to me that this is an area where we have made remarkable progress, all of it good. I did some research to prepare this paper, and found out a few pretty amazing things. For instance, we've only had national free public education for about a hundred years. A hundred years! My mother-in-law is ninety and still going strong. Somehow, having a ninety-year-old in the family makes a century seem short, and so it is if you measure it by anything but the average life span.

Here's another statistic: The very first public high school in America didn't come along until 1821, the first public kindergarten in 1873. And there weren't any free public libraries in this country before the 1850s. We had twenty-one subscription libraries by 1760, but nothing free to the public for another hundred years. The American Library Association wasn't founded until 1876, and there wasn't a single library school in existence until 1887. Seems to me we've done a lot in a hundred years.

Let's see if I can tie all this together. There is a great national outcry these days about a number of issues centered on reading, but in a curious way it's paradoxical. On the one hand we say that the world is changing too fast—let's slow it down. And then on the other hand, we want it to change even faster. After all, my research revealed that as short a time ago as 1900—when my mother-in-law was already four years old—a whopping 10 percent of our population over age fourteen was illiterate. Ten percent! And less than three-fourths of our children age five to seventeen were enrolled in school. Think about that—a full 25 percent of American children not in school at all only eighty-six years ago. That was the good old days? So we have progressed. There can be no question about it. It's just that it seems we don't progress at a steady pace. We slip and slide around a lot.

And so we have this outcry now. It began when we started to suspect that somehow or other our children's reading and writing skills are not what they ought to be, and it's culminating in alarming statistics having to do with current literacy levels. They seem alarming, anyway, if you don't look back to 1900.

We are blaming our children's poor reading and writing skills on television, an easy and pleasant machine, and also on the seductive and mysterious computer, which, I understand, is easy and pleasant, too, though I have so far resisted finding out for myself. There can be no question about the fact that these two inventions are changing our world. They are only the latest things to change our world, which has been in a constant process of change since its creation. But latest or not, they are changing it profoundly. Still, I think it's highly debatable that they are single-handedly responsible for our difficulties. I'm no sociologist, but it seems to me that it's not so much the difficulties that are new as it is our expectations.

I come from a word-loving family, and I married a word-loving man. My children are all word lovers, each in his or her own way. But when I was a child in the good old days, my friends weren't all word lovers, not all book lovers, not all good readers and writers; and this is notwithstanding the fact that my friends and I all went to the same public school, had the same teachers, and were all pretty much at the same economic level. And all were growing up without television and computers. It looks to me as if we simply can't expect a universally high level of enthusiasm about reading. That expectation seems new to me. And, unfulfilled, it carries with it for our teachers a heavy and inevitable load of blame. But there always was and always will be a percentage of children that finds reading stale, flat, and unprofitable.

This is hard to accept in a democracy which states, as one of the self-evident truths, that everyone is created equal. It's a beautiful concept, and we believe it's true from a political point of view, as well as from the point of view of opportunity. Well, we Americans may be born *equal*, but we are certainly born *different*. We don't all want the same things, or value the same things. I've moved around enough to be convinced of the truth of that. And if we—you and I—go on believing that we can, should, and must graduate all children from high school and college into a lifetime of appreciative reading of literature, and a capacity for clear and graceful writing, we will, quite simply, break our hearts.

Do you think I believe that, because I have always loved to read, and because I care about clear and graceful writing, I am somehow the product of a good-old-days perfect education? Nonsense. I have always been a washout at mathematics. I had to take high school algebra twice and was finally allowed to pass only because, my teacher said with a discouraged sigh, at least I was good at drawing. My grades in history were disgraceful; somehow, for me, history was the subject that seemed stale, flat, and unprofitable. I nearly flunked Latin, and *did* flunk my midyear exam in a college course in astronomy. Math, history, science— these things are growing in importance every day, and I am not prepared. I say all this to remind us that there is only so much a good educational system can do, and there is only so far the average brain can go in any field without a basic ability, some level of motivation, and at least a dim grasp of what a given subject will mean to the future. But children are notoriously disinterested in the realities of the future. There's too much of it ahead of them to make it seem important.

Well—still—you will say, correctly, that reading is fundamental. If you can't read, you can't learn history whether it interests you or not. And it is our job to do the very best we can to stimulate as much love of reading as we can. We have chosen our professions because we care about books more than we care about fame and fortune; the vast majority of us are veritable paupers— at least, compared to your average big-league athlete—and we are certainly unsung in the wide world.

But were we more sung in the good old days than we are now? Did people really care more about literature back then? I came across something extremely interesting in my research: a list of annual bestsellers from the beginning of the time when such things began to be tabulated. And I found that in the seventy-five years from 1865 to 1940, children's books were on top a full ten times. "Wow!" I said to myself. "This is significant! People must really have cared about their children's reading back then."

But, looking into it all, I found that, yes, it is significant, but not in the way I expected.

In the first eleven of those seventy-five years, *Hans Brinker, Little Women, Little Men,* and *Tom Sawyer* were all top bestsellers. But those same eleven years saw new novels from Thomas Hardy, Henry James, Leo Tolstoy, and Victor Hugo. Great writers all; they just didn't sell very well.

In 1886, *Little Lord Fauntleroy* took the honors well over Henry James's *The Bostonians* and Robert Louis Stevenson's *Dr. Jekyll and Mr. Hyde.* In 1901, *Mrs. Wiggs of the Cabbage Patch* beat out Joseph Conrad's *Lord Jim* and Theodore Dreiser's *Sister Carrie.* And in 1938, a year that saw new novels from William Faulkner, Graham Greene, Richard Wright, Sinclair Lewis, and Ernest Hemingway, guess what sold best? *The Yearling.*

I'm not saying *Mrs. Wiggs of the Cabbage Patch* wasn't a terrific book. But surely none of us is so fatuous as to think it is a better book than *Sister Carrie* or *Lord Jim.* Remember, we are talking about books bought by adults, not children. *Mrs. Wiggs* is a better book than *Jane Fonda's Workout Book,* yes, but not better than Dreiser or Conrad. It simply won't wash to tell ourselves that *Mrs. Wiggs* sold best because in 1901 people cared more about buying books for their children than for themselves. We have to acknowledge that, in 1901, books like *Mrs. Wiggs* were read by everyone. *Mrs. Wiggs,* like television, was easy and pleasant, especially compared to *Sister Carrie* and *Lord Jim,* which are hard and depressing and make you think. And maybe, since the beginning of time, most of us haven't wanted to think more than is absolutely necessary.

So what are we going to do? We want children to learn to

love reading, but over and above the resistance put up by human nature, there are, today, endless distractions. As if TV and movies weren't enough, now there are those blasted computers, too. And they're not going to go away. My husband has computers in his office, and he has a little machine at home which he uses all the time, doing things that were never necessary before but now seem necessary just because they're possible. This annoys me, but there's no point in being cranky and resistant. Computers are here to stay, just like TV.

The only thing we can do, I guess, is fight fire with fire. Well, let me amend that. The only thing *teachers* can do is fight fire with fire. I would fight fire with fire if I could, but that would mean writing a whole other kind of book, and believe me, if I wrote *Natalie Babbitt's Workout Book*, it would only have one page—one page that said, "Get up from the sofa periodically to let the dog in or out." So teachers are going to have to do the fire-fighting. Somehow they're going to have to find a way to make reading as seductive as its rivals—to make it, in other words, easy and pleasant. Because *that*, it seems to me, is the only thing that was better about the good old days. Books—for me, anyway— were easy and pleasant.

One of the things that made books easy and pleasant was the practice of reading aloud. Almost any writing is easy and pleasant when it's read aloud. My fifth-grade teacher, Mrs. Wilson, read aloud to us every day for the last half hour, and she read aloud for pleasure, hers as well as ours. We weren't tested on the books she read to us. We didn't do projects or write to authors. We just relaxed and enjoyed it. Even the classmates of mine who weren't big readers themselves relaxed and enjoyed it.

Some of the things I hear about that are being done with books in classrooms now make my blood run cold. And would certainly have made my blood run cold in 1941 when I was in the fifth grade. I wish I could believe children are enjoying all those extras hooked onto reading a story, but I'm afraid I think it's pretty unlikely. Books have collected countless barnacles of peripheral stuff these days, and how can that do anything but turn reading into hard work?

It would probably be a good idea to accept the fact that human nature has always resisted hard work, that human nature wants to relax and have fun. I'm not saying we should lower our expectations, exactly. I guess I'm saying that in the good old days, reading *seemed* like fun. So maybe it would be worthwhile to look back at Twain's *Tom Sawyer*, the bestseller of 1876. If Tom could make painting a fence seem like fun, maybe we should take a page from his book. Make reading easy and pleasant, with emphasis on the pleasant. Use a little low cunning. Ease up on the projects, schedule time for reading aloud. Read aloud things that you really like, yourself. Everyone responds to a good story, and that is what good literature really is: a good story, well told. If you don't think you've got any skill for reading aloud yourself, bring in someone from the community to do it, someone without a coo in his or her voice, perhaps an actor from a local little theater. When children can see books as sources of pleasure, I think at least some of them will go on from listening to reading by themselves.

I know a librarian who reads a book aloud only up to the part where the story gets really suspenseful. And then she stops and says, "If you want to know what happens next, you'll have to read this story for yourselves." That is low cunning at its absolute best.

Words, after all, quite apart from their utterly essential and fundamental use for communication—words, after all, can be fun. So what we need to do, maybe, is calm down, forget expecting the moon, and try to give back to reading the pleasure it deserves. I think we can go a long way if we take that route. Honey, you know, is actually good for us nutritionally. So is peanut butter. But they taste so good that we forget about the nutrition. Reading is like that. Or at least it should be. And could be. Maybe. All we can do is try.

Senior year photograph, the Laurel School, Cleveland, Ohio, 1950

" *At my high school graduation, the headmistress said to us, 'Remember, girls, no matter where you go, you take yourselves with you.' That was a shocking thing to hear at the time, when we all wanted to become silk purses and swans—symbols of at least one kind of metamorphosis.* "

Metamorphosis

(*1987*)

It has been my lifelong wish that there was no such thing as change. Outward change, anyway. I like things familiar and predictable. And yet, from the very beginning, my life has been made up of repeated outward changes. I have moved twenty-two times. The humblest dandelion has more tangible roots than I do. But moving is the American way. Nearly all of us had to move from somewhere just to get to America in the first place—we or our forebears.

I wonder sometimes, however, how much we really change inwardly as we go along. I wonder how many of us, in the course of an average life, become something really different from what we were in the beginning. At my high school graduation, the headmistress said to us, "Remember, girls, no matter where you go, you take yourselves with you." That was a shocking thing to hear at the time, when we all wanted to become silk purses and swans—symbols of at least one kind of metamorphosis. But our steely-voiced headmistress was absolutely right. We learn things as we go along, we go through experiences that head us sometimes in unexpected directions, but we are still burdened down with our selves, and respond to all experience in ways that anyone who truly knows us could probably describe as predictable.

I suppose the whole thing comes down to what is meant by the term *metamorphosis*. I went back for a reunion a few years ago to the school with the steely-voiced headmistress—she herself, of course, long gone. My classmates and I all looked hard at each other. Most of us, in spite of the thirty years that had elapsed, looked pretty much the same: that is to say, perfectly recognizable. No problem knowing each other on the street. But the heaviest girl was now thin, while the thinnest was now heavy. I wouldn't have known either of them on the street—unless I stopped and talked to them. Then I would have recognized them easily.

Outward changes. There are plenty of those. I always look with great interest at the makeover stories in the women's magazines whenever I come across one. Mrs. G.K. from Kansas as she looked *before*. Before the hairdresser, the makeup artist, and the dress designer had their way with her. *Before*, she was lank-haired, pale, frumpy, and embarrassed. Then—presto! Mrs. G.K. from Kansas *after*: puff-haired, rosy, stylish, and—embarrassed. I think Mrs. G.K. probably went home to Kansas after this experience, washed out the hairspray, wiped off the makeup, put her old denim skirt back on, and said to Mr. G.K., "It was fun, I suppose, but I just didn't feel like *me*." And Mr. G.K. probably gave her a hug and said, "I like you just the way you are."

It can be unsettling to the people around us if we indulge in too much outward change. My daughter, Lucy, once gave me, for a birthday joke, a curly, short-cropped black wig—a sort of Elizabeth Taylor style. We passed it around and everybody tried it on, even my husband and my two sons. But aside from being funny, which it certainly was, it also had an eerie alienating effect. "Take it off," my son Tom said to me quite seriously, when I was wearing it. "You don't look like my mom anymore."

The wig did represent a kind of momentary metamorphosis, but not a metamorphosis greatly to be desired after all. We grow used to ourselves, the people around us grow used to us, as we grow older. How we look is closely tied to who we are. We come at last, perhaps, to some understanding of our individual essence.

My good friend and collaborator, the poet Valerie Worth, is much concerned with essence. She writes about it often. In one of her collections of poetry, *Still More Small Poems*, she has this to say about a rosebush:

> *In summer it*
> *Blooms out fat*
> *And sweet as milk;*
> *In winter it*
> *Thins to a bitter*
> *Tangle of bones;*

And who can say
Which is the
True rosebush?

A question well worth pondering. But no doubt the rosebush itself knows the answer, just as we know at last our own essence.

I don't suppose there's anyone, and I emphatically include myself, who doesn't wish he were different in some way from what he is. But I doubt if any of us would really be willing to undergo a true metamorphosis now, one that altered our inward essence: to become some new and wonderful other kind of person at the touch of a godmother's wand and then go back to our unchanged lives, the lives that we have shaped—or tried to shape—to fit the person we were before. No, if we underwent a metamorphosis, everything else would have to change as well, or else we would be forced to live as new square pegs in old round holes: uncomfortable, alien, the proverbial odd man out.

But in spite of this, at some level the longing is there, this longing to be different. We say to ourselves that we are the way we are because of things that happened long before we had anything to say about it, and that is probably largely true, though some of what we are is certainly due to the experiences to which life, in its random and disinterested way, has exposed us. Nature and nurture, as the psychologists have it. We say we didn't have much choice, and we also say that we wish we were different. Very different, or maybe only a little different, but different. Younger, perhaps. Or thinner. Richer. Smarter. Even, perhaps, gentler. Or more confident. Or wittier. But most of us adults know by now that we are unlikely ever to be much different. We are, finally, what and who we are, and that's that. Nevertheless—nevertheless—the longing is there, and perhaps that longing is at the bottom of many of the stories we have produced for our children. Unlike adults, children seem to go through changes rapidly and constantly. Outward changes, anyway. They may not be much aware of it, but we, as parents and teachers, certainly are.

Children, however, are born as we were born: each with his or her own essence, an essence that is largely unalterable in spite of continual outward changes. Parents sometimes take a long time to accept their children's essences. If the children don't turn out to be heroes, parents sometimes feel let down. Here these offspring were, beginning new, and they perversely turned out to be just like us. If we could do it over again, *we* wouldn't turn out to be just like us. And yet, Frank Stockton, in his story "The Bee-Man of Orn," reminds us that a reversion to childhood, a new beginning as an infant, doesn't at all mean that we will grow up to be a different kind of adult. The Bee-Man, after his metamorphosis, becomes a bee-man all over again.

But this is not the message of many children's stories. Many stories say, "The power to be whatever you want to be is there for you. You can and will be different." Probably we mean "different from the way we turned out." And sometimes they are different. But the things that make the difference are very seldom in life what they are in stories. In stories the things that make the difference are mostly magic, or obedience to a set of rules, or are due to events carefully orchestrated by the author to produce the desired result. To produce, in other words, a hero.

In *The Secret Garden*, which I loved when I was a child,

Mary and Colin begin their story weak, self-centered, rude, and manipulative. By the time the story is over, they have become wise, sweet, and powerful. In the setting provided for them, and with events carefully arranged, this metamorphosis seems reasonable. I doubt if, given their early experience, so dramatic a change would happen in real life, but who cares? It's a story; and a story, after all, is an acting out of our best-loved dreams and desires. Mary and Colin rebel against authority, take charge of their own lives, and thereby prosper. The concept is irresistible to a child. In a way it's funny that we, as adults jealous of our control, should give such a story to a child, for who among us wants to encourage rebellion? But of course we don't give our children *The Secret Garden* to read because we think they will learn from it. We give it to them because we still remember the magic it worked on us when we were children. And a good thing, too. Otherwise, children would miss out on a great deal of magic.

But an adult rereading of *The Secret Garden* considerably damages its magic. And there are other beloved stories where the magic is equally fragile. *The Ugly Duckling* is one of these, I think. So is *The Little Engine That Could.* Too many of us adults look exactly as we might have been expected to look, given our childhood features. And too many of us have grown up to be little engines that *couldn't,* in spite of the greatest efforts. But I am not saying we are all unhappy and discouraged. Most of us have comfortably accepted the facts of our selves. I'm talking about Mrs. G.K. from Kansas, who realized she didn't really want to be Cinderella after all. We've seen by now too many Cinderellas grown petulant and anxious when their beauty faded with aging. And regardless of our political views, certainly most of us would agree that although Lieutenant Colonel Oliver North is a little engine that could, he will probably end up forgotten on a siding.

But I don't want to be misunderstood. I am not saying that the encouragement of children's hopes for glory through the great metamorphosis of growing up is a bad thing. Not at all. As long as we define glory carefully. Perhaps the best glory of all comes in the form of a sense of the ridiculous, a satisfying kind of daily work to do, and tolerance.

My favorite two books when I was a child were *Alice in Wonderland* and *Alice Through the Looking-Glass*. These books are full of transformations. I loved the pig baby and the Cheshire cat and the Caterpillar. Remember this exchange between Alice and the Caterpillar?

> *"Being so many different sizes in a day is very confusing," [said Alice].*
>
> *"It isn't," said the Caterpillar.*
>
> *"Well, perhaps you haven't found it so yet," said Alice; "but when you have to turn into a chrysalis—you will some day, you know—and then after that into a butterfly, I should think you'll feel it a little queer, won't you?"*
>
> *"Not a bit," said the Caterpillar.*
>
> *"Well, perhaps your feelings may be different," said Alice; "all I know is, it would feel very queer to* me."

Yes, indeed! That seemed like a reasonable reaction to me when I was a child. It seems reasonable now. All of *Alice* seemed and seems reasonable. For Alice wasn't changed at all by her

Wonderland experiences. Alice stayed her own true self throughout. Lewis Carroll didn't want Alice to change. He only wanted to point out, I think, the endless absurdities of the adult world. And maybe that's why I liked the books so much. They seemed to be saying, from Alice's viewpoint, "The world is utterly crazy, but I'm all right." That's the way I felt as a child. It's not a bad way to feel. Perhaps it encouraged tolerance and a sense of the ridiculous.

One of the things that worries me about modern American life is that we are rather short on tolerance. I am not talking about the great political struggles for racial and gender tolerance. I'm talking about the small but precious kind of tolerance that comes from self-acceptance. Not self-satisfaction. Self-*acceptance*. We all seem to think we ought to be like someone else. Look like someone else, live like someone else. Instead of trying to be as good a version of ourselves as we can, we seem to think we ought to be someone else entirely. Everything around us encourages this attitude, an attitude that breeds discontent, self-denigration, and guilt.

Take TV, for instance. Everywhere on television, people are beautiful or wise or witty. And sometimes all three at once. Or if they're comical, they're comical in a lovable way. Movies are a little better, but not much. We know a lot about the real lives of the actors and actresses who play these roles. We know a lot about the lives of our flesh-and-blood heroes, too. Maybe our own lives are less dramatic; maybe we won't get into the history books. But it seems to me it's time we realized that most of us are just as worthy. Maybe we are even more honorable, more unselfish, more loving than many of the celebrities who glitter above our heads.

So why do we wish to be changed into one of their number? In order to be famous? I doubt it. In order to be happy? Probably we don't really believe celebrities are happier than anyone else. In order to be rich? Ah! That may be part of it. To be rich means to be safe, doesn't it? To be rich means to be respectable. At least, if *we* were rich, we'd be safe and respectable.

All this may not seem to have much to do with children's literature. Metamorphosis in that realm is most often about magic, about shape-shifting, about transformation. And all of those things, finally, are about hope: hope for a better life and a better world. Nevertheless, I want to suggest that we should tread carefully.

There is a line somewhere in the blur between fact and fantasy that is extremely hard to pinpoint. One side of that line encourages children to look hard at themselves and the real world around them, to define the genuinely achievable, and to try as hard as they can to do their very best in fashioning for themselves a life that is honest, fulfilling, tolerant, and as comfortable as possible. The other side of that line encourages them to believe that the world somehow owes them wealth and power and happiness without their having to work for it, that the means to wealth and power and happiness are always just around the corner, will come all in a rush, and at a single stroke metamorphose them into the glittering heroes they see in many of their books and movies and TV shows. It is this side of the line that emphasizes the moment of glory, the moment when the world bows and acknowledges herohood. Very seldom does this side of the line recognize that there is a lot of life left after the moment of glory has passed.

Our beloved democracy treads right along that line that is so hard to pinpoint. Yes, it is absolutely true that America is the land of opportunity. But we'd better be sure our children know that "opportunity" means a *chance* to achieve one's ambitions. If one is willing to work hard. And, yes, it is absolutely true that in America anyone can grow up to be president, but the word is *can*, not will. We'd better be sure our children know that while luck is always a factor in how things turn out, there will be no magic, no fairy godmother, no hag on the road with her basket of charms. We'd better be sure they understand that in real life, a metamorphosis is usually so gradual as to be almost imperceptible.

I am talking to myself as much, here, as I am talking to anyone else. I am thinking about my own children as I watch them establishing themselves in their own lives, defining for themselves their own essences, unraveling for themselves the contradictions created by the facts and fantasies that surrounded them when they were genuinely children. They're doing all right, but it's not as easy as they thought it would be. Why do our children think it will be easy? Is it because it looked so easy in the storybooks and on the TV screen? Is it because we, as parents, somehow failed to inform them? Or do all children automatically think it will be easy? I can't remember whether I thought it would be easy or hard. I simply took it for granted that I would grow up to do what I wanted to do. I *am* doing what I wanted to do, but it certainly has not been easy.

I loved fairy tales when I was a child. And I love them now. The concept of metamorphosis is wonderfully compelling. To be different, to solve all problems at the stroke of a wand, to grow up in an instant, to be rich and beautiful and powerful and happy simply by giving the right answer to a riddle! I am the last person in the world to knock fantasy, because the best fantasy is actually a tool for understanding reality. The only idea I want to stress is the idea that we need to be careful to make a balance.

Yes, the very nature of childhood is metamorphic. But the physical, intellectual, and moral changes are not so much alterations, it seems to me, as developments. Given the proper conditions, a morning-glory bud will grow into a blossom, but a morning-glory blossom, not a daffodil. Both are beautiful, but the essence of one is quite different from the essence of the other. I would like to imagine that a morning-glory bud would hope and dream about becoming the best morning-glory blossom there ever was, and not to be discontent, when the moment arrives, that it is not, instead, a daffodil.

I don't know whether I'm making any sense or not. It all seems very clear inside my head, but saying it plainly is another matter altogether. Perhaps an anecdote will help. On a recent school visit, I was asked by a fifth grader if the magic spring water in *Tuck Everlasting* is real. "No," I said, "it isn't real." "But," said the fifth grader, "didn't you ever think that when you described it so well, as if it was real, we might believe you?" I have lain awake nights over this question. Are we somehow implying in our books that the unreal, the impossible, is more greatly to be desired than the real and the possible? Are we maybe whispering that there are instant metamorphoses to be had somewhere, and that everyone can and should be a hero?

I am only trying to say that we had better tread carefully. Let me end with another reference to *Alice*. Do you remember the scene where Alice visits the Duchess? The Duchess is singing a violent lullaby to a baby as she tosses it up and down, and all the while the cook is shaking pepper into a large pot of soup. An argument erupts and the cook begins throwing things at the Duchess and the baby: pots, pans, dishes. Alice, as Lewis Carroll puts it, is in an "agony of terror" for the baby's life, and so, when at last the Duchess flings the baby at her, Alice carries it out into the open air. The baby, over the next few minutes, goes through a metamorphosis. It changes, in fact, into a pig. And here I quote from the story:

> *So she set the little creature down, and felt quite relieved to see it trot away quietly into the wood. "If it had grown up," she said to herself, "it would have made a dreadfully ugly child: but it makes rather a handsome pig, I think."*

I always thought that the baby had begun as a pig, and was only changing back to what it was intended to be. Whether or not this is what Carroll had in mind, I agree with Alice: better, symbolically, a handsome pig than a dreadfully ugly child. As a baby, the creature shrieked and struggled. As a pig, it "trotted away quietly," back to its natural environment.

We were not all intended to be heroes—or swans. If there is any character to emulate in fantasy literature, it is perhaps the Bee-Man. He is entirely contented to have grown up once again into a bee-man. And contentment may well be the richest of all rewards.

Taking questions at a New York City school, 1981

" *Once, on a school visit, I was asked what the message in* Tuck Everlasting *is. I said, as I always do, that I didn't mean it to have any message at all. But a boy stood up and declared with some heat that he didn't care* what *I said,* Tuck *had a message for him, and the message was that you have to pay a price for what you do. A stern message indeed! And a message it wouldn't occur to me to write a book about. Still, that's what* Tuck *meant to this fifth grader.*

"

A Question from Justine

(*1987*)

Storytellers don't always know what they're saying. This is the conclusion I came to after careful consideration of a letter from a little girl named Justine. She asked me, "Do you have to understand your books before you publish them?" It struck me as a very funny question at first, but the more I thought about it, the more penetrating it came to seem. It's the kind of question Lewis Carroll might well have put into the mouth of one of his characters in *Alice in Wonderland*.

Alice in Wonderland is full of things that seem like nonsense until you really think about them. My favorite chapter is the one about the mad tea party. All of it makes me laugh, but after

Justine's letter, there was one particular part that kept coming back to me. You will recall that the Mad Hatter has asked Alice the riddle about why a raven is like a writing desk, and Alice says, "I believe I can guess that." And then the following exchange takes place:

> "Do you mean that you think you can find out the answer to it?" said the March Hare.
> "Exactly so," said Alice.
> "Then you should say what you mean," the March Hare went on.
> "I do," Alice hastily replied; "at least—at least I mean what I say—that's the same thing, you know."
> "Not the same thing a bit!" said the Hatter.

I had probably read the mad tea party chapter a hundred times without stopping to think about what was really being said here. It took Justine's letter to make it all clear to me. I have come to understand that the Mad Hatter and the March Hare are absolutely correct: There is a difference between meaning what you say and saying what you mean. And it's a difference that writers would probably be better off not looking into too deeply. Nevertheless, that's what I'm going to do here—look into it—and we'll see what comes of the exercise.

Now, certainly most writers mean what they say—especially writers for children—if by "say" you mean the message or lesson put forth in a given book. Writers for adults—well, I sometimes have trouble figuring out what some of them are saying. If a critic or a teacher tells me what a particular writer for adults is saying, I'm not only willing to believe him or her, I'm grateful for the information, because sometimes I think there's a conspiracy among writers for adults—especially poets—to make what they're saying as obscure and inscrutable as possible, thereby running counter to the age-old notion that writing is a form of communication. Years ago, when I lived in another place—I have often lived in another place, and not the same other place, either—I belonged to a small group called the Wednesday Afternoon Tea and Poetry Society. There were only six of us, and we read all kinds of poems by all kinds of poets. Once, I remember, we struggled with one by Theodore Roethke which was utterly impenetrable. It was my opinion, finally, that it had to be about a fire in a greenhouse, but we never did know for sure. So it's hard to figure if Roethke really did mean what he was saying.

Writers for children, on the whole, do mean what they say, I think, although storytellers all have to say things they don't *believe* when they write dialogue for the characters who are supposed to be morally unattractive. And they have to do it convincingly, or else those characters will be flabby and two-dimensional. But all that convincing writing doesn't really confuse the issue, because the thrust of the story itself is a guide to figuring out which characters the author is promoting as good, and therefore representative of the author himself or herself, who is, presumably, also good. Or if not good, then at least sincere. So I think you can take it for granted that most of us in the children's field mean what we say.

But—do we say what we mean? Ah—that's the real question. Here's where the whole thing gets murky. I think most of us *think* we are saying what we mean—while we're saying it. But clearly we also say a great many things we don't understand. And if we don't understand what we're saying—if we don't see what it is that's actually going down on the paper—then it's probable that we sometimes turn out to have said a great many things we *didn't* mean. At least, things we didn't mean to *say*.

Are you following this? I'm having some trouble with it myself. Let's see if I can make it more comprehensible. About fifteen years ago, in the journal *The Lion and the Unicorn*, a critic named Hamida Bosmajian, a professor of English at Seattle University in Washington State, published an essay called *"Charlie and the Chocolate Factory* and Other Excremental Visions." It's an absolutely fascinating essay. It says near the beginning, and I quote, "Children's literature is a complicated artistic, psychological, and social phenomenon, in some ways more so than adult literature because the author projects memories and libidinal releases through forms pretending innocence." And then Dr. Bosmajian says, if you'll forgive my being explicit, that Roald Dahl is using chocolate as a symbol for excrement. She says, and I quote, "Children respond gleefully to *Charlie and the Chocolate Factory*, not only because it is a luxurious food fantasy, but also because it is a fantasy of aggression expressed frequently in terms of bathroom humor. This sweet book is quite nasty." And what's more, she says, "Dahl is quite aware of what he is doing."

In other words, Dr. Bosmajian believes that Roald Dahl was saying what he meant. Well—maybe. I didn't know Roald Dahl personally. But somehow I doubt he sat down and said to himself, "Gee, I think I'll write a book in which chocolate will be a symbol for excrement, and I'll make it as nasty as possible, all the while pretending innocently to make it sweet." It seems far more likely to me that Roald Dahl was never consciously aware of what he was saying, if in fact he was saying what Dr. Bosmajian says he was saying.

Unless they get it from the horse's mouth, the fact is that critics and other analytical thinkers can only *assume* that writers are saying what they mean. And another fact is that, based on what I know about my own stories, writers often say things the meaning of which is either totally obscure to them, or utterly devoid of meaning in the first place.

For instance: People sometimes look at me narrowly and say, "All right. Come clean. What is the actual meaning of the fact that the villain in *Tuck Everlasting* wears a yellow suit? You're saying he's a coward, right?" Now, it's true that the word *yellow* suggests a number of things, some disagreeable and some not. But that's not why I chose it. I chose it simply because I needed a two-syllable color, and purple was out of the question. I had to have a two-syllable color because the phrase *man in the yellow suit* is repeated quite often and needs the rhythm that two syllables give it. It makes much better music with *yellow* than it would have with *black* or *gray*. And in addition, in the days in which the story is set—and even now, in the summertime—men did and do sometimes wear cream-colored, yellowish suits. But they never wear purple. Not if they have any sense. So the fact is that the term *yellow* is utterly devoid, here, of any symbolism whatever. People are often disappointed to hear this, but I cannot tell a lie just to please an analytical mind.

On the other hand, in my one novel for adults, *Herbert Rowbarge*, there's a character who's got a neurosis about carpeting. She's afraid it will roll up on her and smother her. My daughter,

Lucy, who is among other things a writer herself, asked me, "Where in the world did *that* come from?" and I had to say I didn't have the slightest idea.

I also have no idea where most of the stuff in my stories about the Devil comes from. When my husband and I, years ago, went to the Weston Woods studio so that he, who reads aloud far better than I do, could record the stories from the first collection, the woman in charge said to me, "You know, I like these stories, but how did you come up with them? You must be really weird!"

Well, what can I tell you? Someone said once that all my stories are about death, one way or another. But if that's so, it's not necessarily what I mean to write about, so I guess I haven't been saying what I thought I meant.

A first-class reviewer said a lot of nice things about *The Search for Delicious* once long ago. She said that Gaylen, the young hero, "symbolically immerses himself in a clear stream and descends into the womblike subterranean world of the dwarfs . . . where every act assumes sacramental value." (That's *sacramental*, not *excremental*.) She suggested that the music and the dancing of the dwarfs is a religious ritual, and that later when Gaylen goes alone into the mountains, he is "experiencing the hero's characteristic withdrawal stage, a time of meditation and acquisition of spiritual wisdom." I liked the sound of that. And in fact, when she put it that way, I could see it was probably true. Also, it made me sound as if I knew what I was doing. But the fact is, I think, most writers do not at all take a scholarly approach to what they're doing, at least not writers of fiction. At least, not writers of fantasy fiction. You can believe what you like, but it seems to me that most just do it from instinct. In other words, if we're saying what we mean, what we mean is something that functions primarily on a subconscious level. So it may be that in some cases, in spite of what I've said above about Roald Dahl and Dr. Bosmajian, a scholar may be better able to say what a writer means than the *writer* is.

But there's plenty of stuff in the subconscious of us all which is far more personal than an inborn understanding of quest patterns and religious symbolism, and here's where I think we are in for trouble. A good deal has been written in recent years about my beloved Lewis Carroll. It appears that he had rather a thing about little girls. It appears that he lost interest in Alice Liddell, the real-life model for his stories' heroine, as soon as she grew up. He liked *little* girls. And he took pictures of them, sometimes without their having any clothes on. I don't know what to make of this. And I don't know if it ought to matter, by which you can tell I'm not a scholar, because from a scholar's point of view it does matter. A scholar would say that understanding a writer's psyche helps to understand a writer's work. This seems to make sense. And, as I've said, it also makes sense that a scholar might sometimes understand an author's work better than the author does. Nevertheless, as a reader, I don't always want to know disagreeable things about the author of the book I'm reading. All I want is the book itself.

A man named Michael Tunnell, who was and maybe still is an assistant professor at Arkansas State University, once wrote an essay about *Tuck Everlasting*. In it he said that I recognize, and I quote, "the universal subconscious fear adolescents harbor concerning parental domination and their inability to achieve independence." This came as happy news to me. I had no idea that I recognized such things. Actually, as a child, I basked in parental domination and had no desire at all to achieve independence. Or so my conscious memory tells me. Even now, as I approach my dotage, I still view independence as a decidedly mixed blessing. And yet, in reading what Mr. Tunnell had to say, I could see that I was saying what he said I was saying. In other words, I was saying what I didn't know I meant.

In thinking it all over, though, it seems to me that in the final analysis, it doesn't matter in the least to the average reader what a writer thinks he has said. A book, once it's published, takes on a sort of chameleonlike character. It becomes something different for each person who reads it, and who's to say that one of these interpretations is more valid than another? Once, on a school visit, I was asked what the message in *Tuck Everlasting* is. I said, as I always do, that I didn't mean it to have any message at all. But a boy stood up and declared with some heat that he didn't care *what* I said, *Tuck* had a message for him, and the message was that you have to pay a price for what you do. A stern message indeed! And a message it wouldn't occur to me to write a book about. Still, that's what *Tuck* meant to this fifth grader. He was doing what all of us do who are not real critics. He was applying his own filters to a story and taking from it what seemed to him to be true and useful. Writers should be grateful when *anyone* can find true and useful things in their stories, whether or not those things were put into the stories on purpose.

So what does it matter what the writer thinks he or she has said? It's quite possible that stories have their own body language and are revealing things their authors didn't mean them to reveal. It just so happens that I do believe, like the fifth grader I just spoke of, that you have to pay a price for what you do, most of the time, whether or not I thought I was saying so in *Tuck Everlasting*.

I once read that when *Ferdinand the Bull* first came out, it got short shrift because it was taken to be a pacifist political statement about the Spanish Civil War. Well, maybe it was and maybe it wasn't. I don't know. My picture book *Phoebe's Revolt* was once reprinted for use in a textbook of some sort, and the people who were doing it felt they had to change a picture where Phoebe's father is helping her out of a bathtub. It made them uncomfortable that she didn't have any clothes on, what with her father right there in front of her. They fixed the picture up by putting a towel around her. I didn't mind this, but the really funny part was that my editor, Michael di Capua, confessed to me afterward that the picture had always made him uncomfortable, too. Not because Phoebe didn't have any clothes on, however. What bothered him was that the position she's in made it look to him as if she's trying to kick her father in the groin. This is certainly not what I meant the picture to say. I think of myself as a feminist, but I have certainly never to my conscious knowledge wanted to kick any of my male relatives, in the groin or anywhere else.

And yet. And yet. How do we know what's going on in our subconscious minds? I'm not, to tell you the truth, a critical reader once you get past misplaced commas and split infinitives. That is to say, I'm not a *scholarly* reader. But when someone who is scholarly points out in an essay that all of L. Frank Baum's male characters in the Oz books are weak, bumbling, and minus some part of their anatomy, while the female characters are brisk, efficient, take-charge types—well, I can see that this is so. It's as plain as the nose on Pinocchio's face. (And a lot has been written about Pinocchio's nose, too, you know, but never mind that.) So, with the Oz books, did L. Frank Baum say what he meant? Or did he say what he didn't realize he meant? Or did he actually mean what he said? Did he really mean to say that males are inferior beings? I find that hard to buy, just as I find it hard to buy another critical analysis, of *Peter Pan* in this case, which claims that James Barrie was saying men don't want to grow up and leave their mothers. Must all literature come down to this? And if it does come down to this, are children picking up all these subliminal messages and being shaped by them?

I can't believe so. If it were all really true, then we would have to have some sympathy for the book banners. I suppose you could find, for every book ever written, someone who wants to ban it. Book banning is an abomination and I don't want to get onto the subject. Suffice it to say that it seems to me children don't automatically pick up the wrong things from a book, however you want to define "wrong." One of my favorite books when I was a child was *The Secret Garden*. But when I reread it a few years ago, I saw that, if looked at through one set of filters, it is full of dangerous stuff. Looked at that way, *The Secret Garden* promotes rebellion against authority. It promotes the idea that not only is it fun to break rules and do things on the sly, but such activities can also be positive and productive. That's not at all what I got from the book when I first read it at the age of nine or ten. What I got from it then was simply that it was a suspenseful story, wonderfully told, in which the heroine was not, thank goodness, a beautiful Goody Two-shoes, but a crabby, self-centered, unbeautiful heroine: a real person and easy to identify with.

So, to wrap it all up, perhaps we can say that regardless of whether writers say what they mean, and mean what they say, readers will take from books what they wish to take, and what they wish to take will not necessarily be what the writers expected them to take.

Do people who write for children really pretend innocence, as Hamida Bosmajian suggested in her essay about *Charlie and the Chocolate Factory*? Perhaps some of us do, though I would prefer to say that we *remember* innocence, and, as the Mad Hatter would say, that's not the same thing a bit. But far more important than what we may project about innocence, I know we do not pretend about hope. Maybe there's stuff in our stories that we don't know or won't admit is there, but the hope is there, all right, no pretense about it: hope for peace, for reason, for justice, for a meaningful life. In this case, if in no other, we mean what we say and are saying what we mean. And maybe, as long as that much is true, it's enough.

Natalie Moore (front row, third from left) with second-grade class at
Lincoln School, Westerville, Ohio, 1939

"*I think a work of fiction, for children especially, needs to present life as it
really is: a mixture of joy and sorrow, of the solvable and the unsolvable,
of the simple and the complicated. I hope my grandchild will be a reader
and that he will learn something about the contradictions of life from books
before he is thrust out to learn the same thing firsthand.*"

The Purpose of Literature— and Who Cares?

(*1989*)

Last summer I gave a speech at the annual children's book conference at Simmons College in Boston, and afterward, during the question-and-answer period, a young woman asked me why I don't write books about the current societal problems of American children. She was especially concerned, she said, about poverty, drugs, and sexual abuse. These were topics, she said, that needed to be treated in books for children because such books could help children to deal with them. My answer was, I'm afraid, rather knee-jerk and glib. "That," I said grandly, "is not the purpose of literature."

I have been thinking about that question, and my answer to

it, ever since. And then, only a couple of weeks ago, in the *New York Times Book Review*, an essay by Mark Jonathan Harris raised it once again. He suggested—and I more or less quote—that "because there are no easy solutions to [social problems], most writers simply avoid dealing with [them]" and warned that "it is critical that we not disdain or ignore the experience of one-fifth of our children." Again I found myself saying, but only to myself this time, thank goodness, "That is not the purpose of literature." But I began to realize that unless I could satisfy myself as to what the purpose of literature is, it wasn't much use to say what it isn't.

By the way, please do not think for one instant that I take lightly the terrible conditions under which so many American children are living. In a time of great change in eastern Europe, with a chance at last for freedom and democracy in places where things have been very dark for a long, long time, we have these sorrows here, and it is difficult to make sense of the contrast. The changes in Europe are new and exciting; the sorrows here are as old as time and as resistant to solution. But the purpose here is not to talk about the sorrows themselves. The purpose is to talk about literature.

One of the things that makes the children's book field different from the adult book field is that there are a number of implied responsibilities for us that are simply never thought of by adult writers. All writers are expected, and rightly so, to keep their work free of any personal racism, sexism, or religious bias. But beyond that, I don't think people who write fiction for adults give much if any thought to being helpful or useful to their readers. The old maxim that says writers should write about what they know is in full sway, just as much as it ever was, and so subjects and settings and points of view are just as varied as they ever were. It's hard to imagine anyone seriously suggesting—in an Authors Guild meeting, for instance—that everyone from Tom Wolfe to Judith Krantz should start writing about poverty and drugs and sexual abuse, even though these terrible problems are making at least as many adults miserable as children. Writers for adults would probably say—though this is only conjecture on my part, since I haven't asked any of them—I would have, but I don't know any—they would probably say that they are writing in response to an inner impulse, as opposed to one or another need on the part of the reading public.

There *have* been books for adults written in direct response to pressing social problems. *Uncle Tom's Cabin* is one. Another is *The Grapes of Wrath*. But there aren't many that have lasted. And there aren't many that are written simply to be sympathetic. They tend to be written out of moral outrage, and they are directed at the general public, the general reader. Their object is to make a noise and bring about social change, and some have been remarkably successful at this. Then, once the problem has either been solved or has faded into unimportance, most of these books disappear. I really don't think John Steinbeck expected migrant workers to read *The Grapes of Wrath* and be comforted by it, any more than Harriet Beecher Stowe expected *Uncle Tom's Cabin* to be read by slaves.

The novels of Charles Dickens have lasted, and you could argue that Dickens always wrote about pressing social problems. But it's not the same thing. He wrote often about the miseries of his own childhood, and in doing so, he was following the maxim: He was writing about what he knew, from his own experience, and his own experience is what brings the passion and the truth to his characters and makes them durable.

But the young woman at the Simmons conference, and Mark Jonathan Harris in his *Times* essay, were not suggesting that writers for children address the general public and raise a cry for change. They were suggesting, unless I misunderstood them, that we write for the children themselves with the idea of bringing directly to them sympathy, encouragement, and the realization that they are not alone. These things are extremely important. They are things that fiction can bring to readers of any age who suffer from any kind of problem. But only if, like Dickens's novels, they are full of truth. Truth would make enormous difficulties for the average writer. What is being suggested is a tall order for those who have not undergone themselves the particular, specific miseries that plague so many of today's children. It requires either a great leap of the imagination on the one hand or, on the other hand, research of a kind to which most writers would be understandably reluctant to submit themselves. It is an order that leads a writer away from the general to focus on the particular— to write directly to the present needs of one segment of the child population, to think specifically of the audience, to find motivation outside his own life. It is an order that could be filled far more effectively and efficiently by social workers and psychologists than by writers of fiction. The world in which we live, which produces the social problems of children, cannot be changed by writers of children's books, because children's books are not read by the general public, and the general public is the only part of the population with the power to make changes. Children have no power.

And there is another uncomfortable piece to this tall order: It may preclude the creation of good fiction. So, well, what is good fiction anyway, and why bother with it when there are children in need for whom it may be useless? Might it not be better to bring to those children some sense that they are not alone, than to worry about creating good fiction? Talk about tall orders! At this point, in preparing this paper, I began to wish I'd chosen to talk about something easy, like fantasy. I'm not a critic, and any definition of literature from me is bound to be as full of holes as an old screen door. Is literature fiction that in some way enlarges the soul, by which I mean that it somehow takes the reader beyond his own life and his own experience and shows him how human beings are alike rather than how they are different? Maybe. A poet, whose name I am sorry to say I cannot remember, said recently on television that if you reach down deeply enough into your own psyche, you come to the place where the things you write about are no longer personal but universal. That was good, I thought. That was maybe a satisfying definition of good fiction: It goes beyond the personal into the universal.

But—what's the use of universals to a child made miserable by the dreary facts of his own immediate existence? Who cares what the soul is doing when the body is besieged by present dangers? Maybe it's a luxury to try to enlarge a soul. Maybe the only souls that can be enlarged are souls in comfortable, well-fed bodies, for there's an old saying that when poverty comes in through the door, love goes out the window. To which I would add that along with love goes philosophy. Maybe those of us who have been fond of saying that all writing is alike, regardless of the intended audience, are full of hot air. It may be true that those who write fiction for adults have no responsibility toward their readers, but it may be equally true that someone who writes fiction for children does have responsibilities and should be drummed out of the field if he doesn't make an effort to meet them.

And yet—you see, I have this deeply held conviction, with no clear idea of where it came from, that you can't write a decent book if the subject or theme is prescribed from the outside, by something beyond your experience and your own truths and passions. And so you can see that for me, all this is difficult and complicated. And in addition to all the stuff about trying to enlarge the soul, and trying to meet the immediate needs of the reader, there is a whole other element which we'd better not forget, and that is that a book has to be a pleasure to read. If a book isn't first of all a pleasure, then it can't do any good no matter how literary it may be or how useful to present needs, because nobody will read it.

Given all these demands, it's a wonder anyone ever undertakes the writing of fiction at all, at least fiction for children. It may in fact be impossible to write a book for children which meets all three of these requirements. It may be impossible to enlarge the soul, meet present and specific needs, and please the reader all at the same time.

In my own case, there is no way to meet with any honesty the present and specific needs of those children referred to by the young woman at the Simmons conference and by Mark Jonathan Harris. I don't avoid dealing with them because there are no easy solutions. I avoid them because I don't know, firsthand, anything about them. On a scale of one to ten, I am a five. I've never been rich, but I've never been really poor, either. The only homelessness I know anything about is the kind you experience in moving, when you've left the old place but are not yet installed in the new. The only drug I've ever struggled with is nicotine. And I've never gone hungry.

There are thousands and thousands of people just like me. But just because we are fives, it doesn't follow that we are innocent lambs, untouched by life. And it doesn't mean that we are numb. We may fall somewhere between the Brontë sisters and Ernest Hemingway in terms of experience of the world, but we are still human. And so, in direct proportion to how long we've been around—well, if you've ever moved, you know how the moving companies rate your furniture on their work sheets before they put it into the van: *chipped, scratched, marred.* And I'm sure we would all like to think that we have learned maybe not a lot, but *something.*

Here is one thing I've learned: My grandson, at fifteen months, brings out in me feelings I was too young and too busy to face with my own children when they were his age. His beauty is humbling; his trustingness, his vulnerability, his very littleness—these things are sometimes almost more than I can bear. Because I know, now, what I didn't really know with my own children: No power on earth can protect him from life. No matter what is done for him, no matter how much he is loved, and educated, and supplied with books and music and attention to the needs of his soul and his body, he is doomed, simply because he is human, to suffer loneliness, disappointment, anger, despair, confusion, and pain. I yearn to protect him, but I know that protection is impossible.

He will share these common human woes with every other child in the world, to a greater or lesser degree, because all are human. But, fortunately, this is not all he will share. He will also share common human joys. For there is joy around, always. It is a blighted life indeed which has never known a joy of any kind, and books are not for lives like that. Those lives need a kind of care and attention no writer of fiction can provide, however well-intentioned.

So I think a work of fiction, for children especially, needs to present life as it really is: a mixture of joy and sorrow, of the solvable and the unsolvable, of the simple and the complicated. I hope my grandchild will be a reader and that he will learn something about the contradictions of life from books before he is thrust out to learn the same thing firsthand.

Thinking about all this, however, brought me no closer to defining the purpose of literature or even what literature is. In desperation, I finally said to my husband—to whom I don't like to admit I am stumped—"Sam," I said, "what is the purpose of literature?" He looked surprised by the question. "Literature has hundreds of purposes," he said. And he should know. He has a PhD in it.

This was plenty discouraging. It threw me right back onto my own recognizance. Once there, I had to admit that what I used to think was the definition of literature is plain and simple twaddle. I used to think that literature was the top layer of fiction— the layer that was going to last, or already had lasted, for generations. Up in that layer was *The Odyssey* and *War and Peace* and *The Golden Bowl* and *Dombey and Son* and—well, you get the gist. I used to think that all writers should strive to create what I was calling literature because everything else was temporary, if not downright trashy. I was wrong. Literature is simply fiction, some good, some not so good, depending on who's doing the choosing, and—it has hundreds of purposes.

It's twaddle to say that writers should sit down and try deliberately to create work of lasting value, and that, by so trying, they should avoid dealing with the social problems of the moment because if they do, their work is doomed to eventual obscurity. If there's anything to be learned in our present-day world, it's that *lasting value* is a term of dubious significance. I've still got my mother's old metal kitchen grater. It has four sides and a handle on top, and you can grate cheese and slice cucumbers with it, and one side has large perforations with such wickedly sharp edges that it looks like a medieval instrument of torture. I don't know what that side is for. My mother probably got this tool when she was married in 1928, so it's sixty-one years old and still going strong. It has survived my mother, and it will survive me. That's lasting value for you. It is still possible to create kitchen tools of lasting value, but nobody, least of all me, can say what will make a work of fiction survive. And even if we could, I defy any writer to create, by an act of will, a work with any built-in guarantee. As a motive for writing, that would be arrogant nonsense. The ages will decide what lasts, not the writer.

So—literature has hundreds of purposes and I for one no longer care. But one question remains: Do we, as writers for children, really have any special responsibility? We do. We have a responsibility to do the very best work we're capable of. And I still think that means we should each stick to what we know, and do what we do best. Some of us will write movingly and effectively about the current societal problems of children and may be able to bring comfort to those children if only by showing them they are not alone. Some of us will write funny books, lighthearted books, and thank goodness for them! Some of us will write about ideas and snippets of philosophy we find puzzling and interesting. Some of us will write about sports, or the solving of cops-and-robbers mysteries, or aliens from outer space, or dinosaurs. All of it will be literature, all fiction. All will serve one purpose or another. Some will be good, some not so good, again depending on who's doing the choosing. But, for pity's sake, let us hope that these books will first and foremost bring pleasure to their readers, regardless of which of the hundreds of purposes they serve, because otherwise it won't matter what they're about, or whether they're good or not so good, and it won't matter whether a given writer spent ten weeks or ten years writing one of them, because no child will bother to read them. And if a child is forced to read one in school, he will forget it as quickly as possible afterward.

Maybe, after all, there is one single purpose for literature—one foremost purpose, anyway. Maybe the giving of pleasure is the purpose. I find I could care about that. The purpose of literature is to give pleasure to the reader. I will leave it to somebody else to define what pleasure is. It could be a topic for some other paper: What is the purpose of pleasure? I hope nobody will ask me to deal with it.

The truth is that Mylo was very much afraid of the dark.

Illustration from *The Something* (1970), with a sketch for type treatment

" *We have always dealt with [fear] by giving it human form and naming it. If it's named and given a shape, we can deal with it. That is how storytelling began, and that is what storytelling still is, even after centuries. Telling stories is one of the most civilizing things we do. Externalize the fear, bring the dark out into the light and look at it and memorize its features so you will know it when you meet it next time.* "

Darkness and Light

(*1990*)

I 've been doing a lot of thinking lately about dark and light. Some of this is because it's November. November is not my favorite month. Winter is not my favorite season. But another part of the reason comes out of talk from our presidential candidates about hope and fear, and about leaving the world a better place for our children and grandchildren to grow up in. Of course we want very much to give them hope and we would like very much to make their fear as small as possible in these hard times. There have been hard times before, though. I was born in the worst of the Great Depression, but somehow managed to grow up with plenty of hope. It's easier to feel hopeful in good times than in bad, certainly. It's easier to feel hopeful in May than it is in November. But somehow there mostly seems to be enough hope to tide us over. What we need is a balance, and a sense of balance comes from rational thinking. Rational thinking is, I like to imagine, the best end product of being civilized. I want to try to make sense of this here, for you and for myself, because it's a topic worth talking about for people who are interested in children. People who work for and with children—parents, teachers, librarians, writers, illustrators, and all the various sciences, too—all of us are doing, at bottom, the same thing: We are trying to civilize the next generation.

There are a lot of different ways to define what *civilizing* means, but one meaning certainly is that we are trying to prepare children to function well in the society in which they will most likely live. Of course, it's work full of frustration and uncertainty, today more than ever, because we don't really know anymore what society will be like at any particular point in the future. It changes constantly. It has always been in a process of change, but in recent decades the process seems to have accelerated. Nevertheless, whether we are frustrated or not, we must make the effort.

It's interesting that human beings are born so uncivilized— are born without any idea at all about how to function successfully. I have a granddaughter now. She's two and a half. She is utterly uncivilized. She does appalling things with food and drink. She is noisy in public places. She hasn't an iota of consideration for other people, and no concept at all of give and take. We're all absolutely crazy about her. Her dark side is as much on the surface as her light side. She will pat your cheek and then pinch you painfully on the nose. Her beautiful little face is a mask of tragedy one minute and a mask of comedy the next. And then there are times when she simply sits and muses, gazing off into space like Charles Dickens's wonderful Captain Bunsby, who, even in port in London, always seemed to have "his eye on the coast of Greenland." She is going to be what they call a "handful." Civilizing her will not be a task for sissies.

And yet I have seen domestic kittens, and so have you, whose eyes have barely opened but who are already well on the way to good functioning in *their* society. In eight weeks they'll be on their own. Baby animals in the wild are trained by their mothers to hunt and survive, but the process rarely takes longer than a year. It's different with humans for a great many reasons, but at least in part because of our complex brains and our complex societies. Our babies must be taught to survive on many different levels, and they must be taught self-control of a sort that kittens, tame or wild, never have to bother with. We are concerned, those of us who work with and for children, to teach those children moral and philosophical survival as much as, if not more than, any other kind. We want them to be morally and philosophically courageous because we know that at the bottom of every cruel or immoral act, there is fear. And cruel, immoral acts upset the delicate balance of our society.

It seems to me that we are full of fear, we humans. It's natural, but it's dangerous. Unlike other animals, who don't know and don't care, we are painfully aware that we have no hard evidence about where we came from or where and when we're going. So we live in a constant state of apprehension, consciously or unconsciously, and that sometimes makes for irrational behavior. Over the centuries we have invented and discarded and reinvented countless systems to answer our questions, shore up our hopes, and keep our societies functioning. Some of these systems are pretty wild: voodoo; animal sacrifice; self-flagellation; astrology; numerology; burial of the dead in trees, in jars, in pyramids; oracles; rabbit's feet; face-lifts; knocking on wood. These things are charms to light up the dark. For the dark means the unknown and the unknown means danger, and danger is synonymous with fear.

In civilized societies—and by that I mean civilized as we like to define it, though the word has many different interpretations—bees in their way are civilized if by that you mean individuals working for the good of the group—but, anyway, in civilized societies we do two things to control fear and promote moral and philosophical survival: We invent rules for behavior, and we externalize fear as much as we can so that it seems visible and controllable. This is right and that is wrong, we say to our children, hoping they will learn moral survival. And—this is good and this is evil, we say to them, hoping they will learn philosophical survival. And by doing this we create an uneasy but maintainable balance. Things happen to upset the balance all the time. Small things, big things. A girl is raped and beaten in Central Park. An army officer tells lies. A president is shot. We rock and wobble for a while. Some of us ask hard questions about the value of a system where such things can happen. *Children*, the very children we are trying to civilize, ask hard questions. But after a while the balance is restored. Time helps. Hope helps. We settle down and go on with our lives. But the balance is always uneasy. I think it is like one of those nursery toys with a round, weighted bottom. You poke it and it teeters and rolls like a drunken man—and then it rights itself. It always rights itself.

Even when the balance is maintained, however, there is still fear. We have always dealt with it by giving it human form and naming it. If it's named and given a shape, we can deal with it. That is how storytelling began, and that is what storytelling still is, even after centuries. Telling stories is one of the most civilizing things we do. Externalize the fear, bring the dark out into the light and look at it and memorize its features so you will know it when you meet it next time. And if you have learned the rules for moral and philosophical survival, you will know what to do, how to behave, how to fight, and how to regain your balance.

It's no accident that *dark* has long been the word used to describe evil and danger. It has to have come out of prehistoric feelings about night—a time of risk when you couldn't see your enemy coming. And words related to *dark*—words like *shadow* and *gloom* and *shade*—are common in phrases about frightening things. *The valley of the shadow of death*, for instance. *The dead of night*—that's a good one. Poets have used the word *shade* to mean a ghost. And logically we have used *dark* words to describe ignorance, while wisdom is related to *light*. The Dark Ages, for instance, as opposed to the Age of Enlightenment. One of my favorites comes from my Ohio childhood: My father would say, if someone made a stupid or uninformed remark, "You talk like a man up a dark tree." *Dark* is used as a synonym for blindness, also. It's interesting about that. Physical blindness has absolutely nothing to do with morality. But language takes its metaphors where it finds them. In Dickens's *A Christmas Carol*, a seeing-eye dog pulls its charge out of Scrooge's way on the street as if to say, Dickens suggests, "No eye at all is better than an evil eye, dark master!"

If dark is the absence of light, shadow is darkness in the presence of light, so it's a little different, if you want to be literal. But metaphorically, dark and shadow are the same thing. Dark is the other side of light. Dark and light are fraternal twins, and inseparable as the two faces of Janus, but in storytelling we can and do separate them and let them fight it out for control and supremacy.

Where storytelling is concerned, the dark side is indispensable. Where would a plot be without the villain? Villains are easy to spot in fantasies, for fantasy is an ancient story form that has its roots in the deliberate and often transparent attempt to name and control evil. In fantasy, the hero is pure good, the villain pure evil, and good always wins. Fantasies written for children are the easiest to take because they have child heroes, and we like the notion that children are born pure and good, in spite of the concept of original sin and in spite of the fact that we know children are born neither good nor evil but merely neutral. If this were not the case, we wouldn't have to work so hard to civilize them.

Adult heroes who are pure and good, like Lancelot in the King Arthur stories, tend to be rather irritating. They're not like anyone *we* know. The adults *we* know, emphatically including ourselves, are at least a mixture. But storytellers *have* managed to create a few pure adult heroes who, even if they are without sin, are at least charmingly bloodthirsty where the destruction of villains is concerned. And sometimes they have bad habits.

Western marshals frequently chew tobacco and spit, for instance. Sherlock Holmes is a drug addict. And Dickens is chock-full of secondary heroes like Mr. Micawber, who are deeply flawed and yet can save the day with the best of them. Dickens does, however, nearly always provide a primary hero who is pure as the driven snow and relentlessly sinned against by large numbers of irredeemable villains. Dickens does villains better than anyone. He'd never have gotten anywhere without them. And he destroys them better than anyone. If you've never read *Dombey and Son*, I urge you to do so if only to see the horrifying and magnificent and utterly just destruction of the villain, Mr. Carker.

But it's been a long time since anyone wrote a novel for adults where the hero is pure good and the villain pure evil. You see the convention occasionally at the movies these days, or on TV, but rarely in a serious novel. It's not fashionable anymore, at least for adults, to misrepresent what we knew all along: that good and evil, dark and light, coexist in us all.

In books for children, however, the convention rolls along as merrily as ever, at least in fantasies. Noble innocence for heroes, foul purposes for villains. All very neat and satisfying.

An interesting exception is Maurice Sendak's *Where the Wild Things Are*. Whether or not Sendak knew what he was doing in that book—as a writer myself, I know that writers aren't always aware of what they're doing—anyway, whether he knew it at the time or not, Sendak was creating something very unusual when he wrote about Max, because Max is a mixture of good and bad in his real world—he is a real, ambivalent child—but when he goes to the place where the wild things are, he becomes a classic fantasy hero. He fights the demons of his subconscious, as Joseph

Campbell would put it, and wins. Then he comes back again and, we like to think, will be a normal good-bad child all over again. Librarians and teachers and parents were nervous about Max at first—nervous about a story in which a child hero behaves badly. But children have always seized on Max and taken him to their hearts. Of course they love the pictures. Of course the happy ending is satisfying. But I think they love best the fact that Max is a mixture of good and bad, just like themselves.

Because we are all of us in the business of trying to civilize our children—to give them guideposts and road maps and systems and labels to help them become balanced adults capable of maintaining the balance of our societies—we are, in spite of Max, uneasy about admitting to children that dark is inseparable from light, that bad is inseparable from good. Maybe, we wonder, if we tell children it is in the nature of humans to be both things at once—an ethical hot fudge sundae, if you will—maybe we will be telling them that it's all right once in a while to be cruel and immoral. It's never all right to be cruel and immoral, no matter how natural the impulse may be. But on the other hand, shouldn't we be willing to admit that bad feelings—angry feelings that make us want to lash out—are all right? Or natural, anyway? As long as we keep them under control?

Dickens's primary heroes and heroines almost never seem to have bad, angry feelings. They nearly always leave the punishment of villains to secondary characters, or to heaven itself, and in a Dickens novel, secondary characters and heaven itself are more than ready to oblige, sometimes in wonderfully imaginative ways. But life is not a novel by Dickens, and we are not heroes and heroines except possibly to ourselves. We are not, and children are not. So how do we teach children to face and control their fear and anger? How do we teach them that their dark side is normal, not "bad," so that they can be generous and forgiving with themselves and other people?

It isn't easy. I went to a series of very unhelpful Sunday schools which managed to confuse me and which taught me guilt instead of love. It seems to me now that my Sunday schools set up impossible goals and then made sure I knew I'd be kept out of heaven if I didn't achieve them. My Sunday schools implied that if you had a dark side, it was there because you deliberately allowed it to be there. You *chose* it. You opened the door of your soul and invited the Devil in. My reaction to this was not alarm, however. I don't know why not. All I remember is that somehow or other, I simply decided it was silly. I think books helped to lead me to that conclusion. Fairy tales and Greek myths and *Alice in Wonderland*. My favorite fairy tale, "Graciosa and Percinet," had a bumbling—if beautiful—heroine who was always doing the very thing she was told not to do. But Percinet loved her anyway. That was very nice. In my favorite Greek myth, the one about Jason and the golden fleece, characters did all kinds of terrible things, but it was the gods who led them to it. It was all laid out ahead of time by all those planners and meddlers on Mount Olympus. And *Alice in Wonderland* was the best of all. Alice is a good-bad child, like Max. But, oh, the adults who populate Wonderland! Rude, sarcastic, short-tempered, quick to get their feelings hurt, irrational, full of senseless advice. Alice stands up to them. She doesn't let them push her around. When the King of Hearts notices in the trial scene that Alice has begun to grow, he reads from his book:

"Rule Forty-two. All persons more than a mile high to leave the court."

Everybody looked at Alice.

"I'm not a mile high," said Alice.

"You are," said the King.

"Nearly two miles high," added the Queen.

"Well, I shan't go, at any rate," said Alice: "besides, that's not a regular rule: you invented it just now."

"It's the oldest rule in the book," said the King.

"Then it ought to be Number One," said Alice.

How I gloried in that exchange when I was a child! I still glory in it.

The *Alice* books don't deal overtly with the dark side of our natures, but it is always implied, sometimes painfully, as in the scene with the fawn in the wood where things have no name. I understood it. I recognized it. The books I liked best did not *inform*; they *confirmed* what I already knew perfectly well by the time I read them. Children learn a great deal from observing adults and other children and, I suppose, themselves as well. If their books are not honest, they will not like their books.

And yet we have to draw a line. And that is very hard to do. How much of life's casual cruelty and injustice must a child see in order to be well armed but not made cynical or thrown into despair? For storytellers it's a special problem, no less for writers of fantasy than for writers of realistic fiction. Gone are the days when all a children's writer had to do was lay out the proper path and move his hero down it, strewing villains behind him as he went, thereby showing young readers how to live. Who knows anymore whether life was really simpler in those days? Maybe it was, so that moralistic, protective storytelling fit right in. But maybe it *wasn't*, so that moralistic, protective storytelling did more harm than good, if only in boring its readers into a stupor. We need to remember that the children in Dickens's novels live in an England very different from the one Kate Greenaway shows us, in spite of the fact that these two authors were writing at more or less the same time. Certainly there were *some* hard truths that children in the 1800s could not escape. Today there are certainly many. Children always knew sometime before the age of ten that death was a certainty—their own and that of the people and animals around them. Certainly they know it now just as early. Casual cruelty and injustice have always been a part of children's lives, back to Dickens, back to the very beginning. So we cannot protect them from the dark side. And if we cannot protect them from it, then perhaps we can help them to accept it and be strong in the face of it.

This next may sound like a contradiction, but I have always thought we human beings take ourselves much too seriously. An article in *Time* magazine, talking about the sun, said that someday, when it runs low on hydrogen, it will swell into a red giant and incinerate our planet. This won't happen for about five billion years, but it's coming. Scientists agree on that. Shouldn't the fact inform our philosophies? Shouldn't it show us how utterly unimportant we are? For there is nothing at all we can do about the sun. Or about storms, or meteor showers, or ocean tides, or tornadoes, or any other phenomena that nature creates according to laws of its own. Nature is neither good nor bad; it simply exists, and we humans are a very small part of it—the only part that has choices to make, the only part with a separate dark and light side. If we could only be taught to accept ourselves as unimportant, we could control our huge egos and learn how to fit in with natural systems both internal and external.

The stories I always liked best were the stories which presented life as it really is: the dark and the light all mixed up together, coexisting, with unanswerable questions remaining unanswered, retaining their mystery and their wonder and their endless power to motivate. If life consisted only of the known and good things, if there were no dark to confront and fight, how dull and uninspiring everything would be! I wouldn't give two cents for a children's book—or any other kind of book—that tells the reader that life is a bowl of Häagen-Dazs ice cream and that bad feelings are alien and can be shed forever, simply driven out of one's heart and mind at will. I knew when I was eight that this is ridiculous. Most of us did, if we would only admit it. And I've always been glad that it's ridiculous. I've had a lucky external life; I know that and am grateful for it, up to a point. But my head is like everyone else's from here to Bangladesh: full of demons and dark places and vague but dangerous notions. We're all the same inside our hearts and minds, and stories that tell the truth about that are loved by us all, all around the world. The truth is pretty simple, after all. It is summed up beautifully in a poem called "Desiderata" written by Max Ehrmann in 1927. Many of you are familiar with it, I'm sure. In part, "Desiderata" says:

*You are a child of the universe, no less than the trees
and the stars; you have a right to be here. And whether
or not it is clear to you, no doubt the universe is*

unfolding as it should . . . Whatever your labors and aspirations, in the noisy confusion of life keep peace with your soul. With all its sham, drudgery and broken dreams, it is still a beautiful world.

Here are all the clues anyone needs for storytelling. You are a child of the universe—yes, part of it, and no more or less important than other parts. The universe is unfolding as it should—yes, and will do so whether or not people can discover motives and reasons, so we might as well relax about it. And, yes, in spite of everything, it is still a beautiful world. That is the most important part to remember and to tell about in stories. That is the way around cynicism and despair. It doesn't deny the dark; it simply reaffirms the light. Not a half-bad way to go forward.

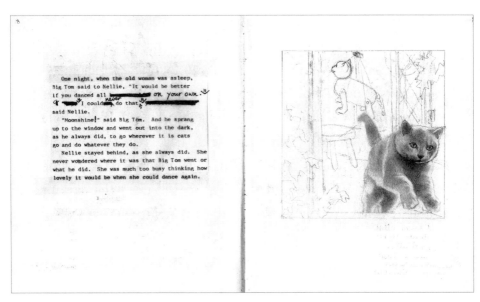

One night, when the old woman was asleep,
Big Tom said to Nellie, "It would be better
if you danced all ~~~~~~~~~ on your own.
~~~~ I could never do that,"
said Nellie.
"Moonshine!" said Big Tom. And he sprang
up to the window and went out into the dark,
as he always did, to go wherever it is cats
go and do whatever they do.
    Nellie stayed behind, as she always did. She
never wondered where it was that Big Tom went or
what he did. She was much too busy thinking how
lovely it would be when she could dance again.

From the dummy for *Nellie: A Cat on Her Own*

" *Children are fundamentally pragmatic, and what they don't see value in,
they will reject. I took a copy of my picture book* Nellie: A Cat on Her Own
*to the four-year-old son of a friend the other day. 'Do you like cats?' I
asked him as I handed him the book. 'No,' he said, and dropped the book
on the floor. Enviable honesty!* "

Protecting Children's Literature

(*1990*)

Ifeel protective about children's fiction, and I also feel protective about the pleasure it's supposed to provide. I think that a lot of what's happened to it lately threatens it. A great deal is being piled on it—things that don't have much to do with the joy of reading—and that's a worry. Fiction is a fragile medium; a good story can collapse if it's made to bear too much weight.

Many of us, in literature classes in college, had to go through the agonizing business of dismantling a novel in order to examine it critically. It was like taking apart a car engine and laying out the pieces on the floor of the garage. It utterly ceases to resemble a car engine and becomes a jumble of seemingly unrelated parts. Not that I've ever taken apart a car engine, mind you, but I once watched a clever niece do it, so I can claim some validity for the metaphor. Sometimes, in those literature classes, stories were put back together in such a way that the pleasure they gave in the beginning was lost forever. Still, it's perfectly true that once a piece of fiction leaves its author's hands, it becomes the property of each person who reads it, and each person will see different things in it, often things the author didn't necessarily intend. So there's no point in the author insisting on a single set of directions for assembly and operation. No point in being possessive. However, feeling possessive about one's own fiction and feeling protective about the whole body of fiction are two very different things.

I know that there is a movement underway to stop using texts for the teaching of reading and to start using works of fiction. In the beginning that seemed to me to be a good idea. But now I'm not so sure. The texts had related workbooks with sentences to complete, quizzes, questions to think about, and all kinds of suggested projects. The feeling, as I understand it, was that these texts and workbooks were making a dry and tedious thing out of learning to read at the very time when concern about literacy levels was growing more and more serious. So it seemed sensible to try using real stories in the classroom—stories that could grab the children's fancies and show them what the joy of reading is all about.

But what I see happening now is that these real stories are being used in the same way that the old texts were used. Every once in a while someone sends me something meant to accompany a classroom reading of my story *Tuck Everlasting*, and here's what I find: a related workbook with sentences to complete, quizzes, questions to think about, and all kinds of suggested projects. I worry that this will make a dry and tedious thing out of fiction. It's as if the same recipe for stew were being followed in both cases, except that chicken has been substituted for hot dogs.

Well, I'm not a teacher, but I can imagine how painfully difficult it must be to try to teach a roomful of kids how to read. And not only how to read but what to read, while at the same time struggling to keep the process reasonably entertaining. The burden teachers have been forced to take on in the last decade or two is truly staggering. And now we've come reeling away from a governors' conference where the glad tidings were announced that we will have 100 percent literacy in this nation by the year 2000. What did they think they were doing? I found it all astonishing and, I must say, irritating. No mention of money being provided for such a horrendous undertaking. No mention of who would be expected to undertake it. Of course, we all know who's expected to undertake it: our teachers. But the governors didn't say how to do it. What the governors did, at least in the television reports I saw, was to emerge from their meetings flushed and starry-eyed with noble purpose, and simply announce that in ten years there will be no more illiteracy. It seems to me you might as well announce that in ten years there will be no more salt in the ocean.

This is not to say that 100 percent literacy isn't something to strive for; but surely, in a sprawling democracy like ours, it's an impossibility. Isn't it? Well, perhaps it depends on what you mean by literacy. And there is something heartbreakingly American about the aspiration. We have always believed we could do anything if we set our minds to it. Just pass a law, and the problem, whatever it may be, is solved automatically. When it doesn't work—and it very often doesn't—we are baffled and outraged. We want things to be perfect.

One of the paths we see as leading to a perfect society is to catch the children early and get them to think about things in the right way. We have all been struck with horror at the truly awful things some of our young people have been doing lately. Drug dealing, murder, rape, random violence with nothing personal in it at all that anyone can see. They are doing things that are not so much immoral as amoral. The implication with immorality is that it is behavior performed in opposition to morality, which implies an understanding of morality. But amoral behavior implies no such understanding. Often it isn't even angry. It is random behavior performed in an emotional vacuum, and it makes a chaos of society. Clearly something has to be done and done without delay if we are to save our children from growing up with no sense at all of social responsibility.

Social responsibility means, to me, caring about others, obeying the laws, keeping the wheels of society oiled and turning, understanding how our personal behavior affects our environment. We learn the basics of it mainly from our parents and siblings, before we ever enter a classroom. I do not think literature can or should be expected to teach it, and I will try to explain why I feel that way.

Let us go way, way back to Oog and Mog, my favorite cavemen, at a time during the thawing of the Ice Age. Oog has just clobbered a musk ox. Mog comes along and wants the musk ox for himself, so he bops Oog over the head with a club. Oog is understandably annoyed. He bops Mog back. "Ow!" says Mog to himself. "That hurts! If I bop Oog again, he'll probably bop me again, and that will hurt, too. So if I don't want to get hurt, I guess I'd better stop bopping." And so social responsibility was born. But it was not born out of consideration for one's fellow man; it was born out of the desire not to get bopped. It appears to me, as this little prehistoric morality play I've just presented shows, that social responsibility is a learned thing arising from the instinct for self-preservation. Consideration for one's fellow man is not instinctive. It has to be demonstrated as wise and useful if one wants to be comfortable. It is, at bottom, selfish.

Now, you would think, wouldn't you, after all the centuries that have passed since Oog and Mog, that human beings would have adapted genetically somehow, and would now be born knowing they had better not go around bopping people. But, alas, this is not the case. My grandson is eighteen months old. He has all the external attributes of an angel, and this is not just the blind raving of your average grandmother. But when he comes to my house to visit, as he does very often, and sees our middle-aged golden retriever, a certain unnerving light comes into his eye. He will give a laugh like that of an imp from hell, pick up a toy, and bop the poor dog with it. And then he will laugh again. He finds her funny to look at, and even funnier to bop. He has no conception at all of kindness and consideration. Not even as much as the dog has. He will have to learn it, like everyone else. It would speed things up if Rosie, our dog, were to bite him, but she won't. She's already learned about biting and bopping. And anyway, my grandchild doesn't know he's doing anything wrong. He is amoral, as we all were at his age. Oog and Mog and all of their descendants, down to you and me and my grandchild, have had to learn social responsibility for the most pragmatic of reasons: to preserve our own comfort and our own skins.

But what about the people who haven't learned it? What about adult criminals guilty of vicious crimes? Why has their amorality survived well past their adolescence? We can only presume it is because they have grown up in a place where people have been bopped whether they bop back or not. And there are, of course, all varieties of bopping. You can be bopped in the spirit, the ego, the heart, as well as on the head. If other people have never cared about you, you're not going to learn how to care about *them*.

Our lives are full of minor examples. One of the least important but most annoying is that of the grocery store fast-checkout lane. EIGHT ITEMS OR LESS is the way it's labeled at my grocery store. But there are people who constantly go through with more than eight items. They go through with two times eight, three times eight. Once or twice I've mentioned the infraction mildly to the culprit, but the culprit is liable to turn surly if you say anything. Liable, in fact, to bop. Once I even said something to the checkout clerk. "Come on!" he said. "It's only a grocery store!" True. But where is the line between the eight-items violation and murder? I'm serious. There has to be a line somewhere, and I want to know where it is. When does it begin to matter whether you obey the rules or not? In my neighborhood, it evidently comes somewhere beyond red lights and stop signs. I complained about this once to a taxi driver. He drew himself up and said proudly, "Rhode Islanders don't like laws."

Clearly, things are out of control around the edges, and something has to be done. Or else I'm getting old and cantankerous. Well, I *am* getting old and cantankerous. Still, steam should be reserved for issues more worthy of the energy. Like, for instance, preserving what little is left of the pleasure of reading fiction. On the face of it, there wouldn't seem to be much of a relationship between eight-items-or-less and curling up with a good book. Well, that's the point. There isn't any connection, and if we try to create one, it's the book that will suffer. Or at any rate, that's my fear.

I don't believe in using fiction to teach anything except the appreciation of fiction. At least, not to children. It seems to me that there is enough difficulty getting them to read in the first place, and the more lessons you clog up reading with, the more of a lesson you make of it. Book discussions are a good thing because everyone needs help in learning to read critically—or perhaps I should say, in learning to think critically. And if a given piece of fiction deals with a particular problem of being human, then it is only natural that the problem be dealt with in the discussion. I know that *Tuck Everlasting* suggests some moral problems, and it's perfectly reasonable to talk about those in a book discussion. But, you know, it's interesting to see, from the letters I get, which of those problems really interest children. Curiously, no child has ever written to me about whether or not Mae Tuck should have killed the man in the yellow suit. They always write about whether or not Winnie Foster should have drunk the spring water and gone off with the fascinating Jesse Tuck. They seem to feel that the man in the yellow suit, like the Wicked Witch of the West, needed killing, and so it's all right. The killing has bothered some grown-ups, but the children don't seem to turn a hair over it. They also do not write to me about whether Winnie did the right thing in helping Mae Tuck escape from jail.

Now, surely these two things, both genuine crimes in our society, are examples of social irresponsibility from which we scarcely want our children to learn. In fact, *Tuck Everlasting* demonstrates, if it demonstrates anything at all, the complicated moral ambiguities of social responsibility. I didn't think about demonstrating anything while I was writing it, though. I only wanted to tell a story and at the same time explore for myself the question of what eternal life might really be like. A lot of children write that they don't agree with me that it would be terrible. In some classrooms they write their own endings for the story. That's perfectly all right with me. What isn't perfectly all right is when they write to tell me, always rather woodenly, what they "learned" from the story. I know these recitals are not from their own hearts. It's easy to tell. The most common expression of it I get is that a child will say, *I learned that living forever would be a bad thing.* And then, in an impassioned postscript, add: *But why didn't Winnie drink the water?*

The best letters of all come from the children who got involved in the story, caught up in what suspense there is, and wanted to see what would happen next. Just normal, everyday fun from a story, the kind we all get with a book we like. Not, you understand, that I imagine they all like *Tuck.* It often takes real persistence on the part of the teachers to get them past the beginning, which a great many children find boring and confusing, and don't hesitate to say so in their letters. But some do like it, thank goodness. And what they take away with them when they've finished it will depend on each child's personal needs and personal quirks. It does appear that a good many of the girls take away a desire to meet a Jesse Tuck, but that's all right. Nothing the matter with romance.

But I don't think any of them are coming away with a heightened sense of social responsibility. They could be made to, of course. You can come away from any book with that, if it's thrust upon you. But how sad for the book! Imagine teaching *Peter Rabbit* that way. Imagine teaching *The Secret Garden* that way. Or *Alice in Wonderland*, or any of the best-loved children's stories. Why do we remember these tales our whole lives long? What is it in them that endears them to us? Certainly it isn't because they taught us to be socially responsible.

I think the single most attractive quality of the stories that have lasted is that their heroes and heroines defy authority and not only get away with it but also create positive and happy endings thereby. To defy authority is to be socially irresponsible, isn't it? But, you see, children are small and surrounded by rules and restrictions and caveats and coercion. Their longing for independence and self-determination is very strong. So is their passion for justice, which they see little enough of, by their lights, in the world around them. If we leave them alone to identify with Alice, with Peter, with Mary and Colin, and with all the other storybook rebels, we are allowing the books to work the magic of identification, and spread the balm of good therapy on their bruises. A good children's book says to the reader, "Yes, Virginia, you *can* escape the pinches of your life and, for a little time, make a difference in the world, even if it is only vicarious." If we turn children's stories into handbooks for proper behavior, we will subvert their purpose and destroy their magic, and do the one other thing which is the saddest of all: make of reading a chore, a drag, just another lesson. And when that happens, the joy of reading evaporates.

I tried hard to think of a beloved children's story that demonstrates social responsibility as a natural part of its action, and I couldn't think of a single one. Every one of the most popular stories I could come up with demonstrated some kind of rebellion along with the need to destroy villains. This was not a surprise to me, though I suppose it's entirely possible that I couldn't find what I was looking for because I didn't want to find it. It's certainly true that children's stories have been written specifically to teach beneficial things. But mostly those stories don't last. Adults may see value in them, but children don't. Children are fundamentally pragmatic, and what they don't see value in, they will reject. I took a copy of my picture book *Nellie: A Cat on Her Own* to the four-year-old son of a friend the other day. "Do you like cats?" I asked him as I handed him the book. "No," he said, and dropped the book on the floor. Enviable honesty!

I would like to say again, flatly, that I think social responsibility comes only from practical experience. I believe in Oog and Mog and the lessons about bopping. Oog and Mog did not need storybooks. I learned about bopping from my sister, not from reading. I read all through my childhood, but the only thing I learned from books was the joy of reading. I rejected stories, like *The Water-Babies* and *Pinocchio*, that attempted to teach me how to behave. I relished the stories, like *Alice in Wonderland* and *Mary Poppins*, which confirmed my belief that breaking other people's rules is a fine thing when good things come of it. But I didn't go around, therefore, in my real life, breaking rules. As children go, I was a very good child. If my mother had told me to stay away from the secret garden, it would still be a tangle of weeds today. But I broke rules along with my stories' heroes and heroines on a regular basis and got a great deal of vicarious satisfaction from it.

Yes, our society is messy; yes, our children need to learn to care for each other and to be, in short, socially responsible. But in all our zeal, I hope we can find a way to teach them without destroying more than we create. I hope our teachers will find a way to keep on reading great children's stories aloud in their classrooms for no other purpose than the joy those stories will bring. I hope the subsequent book discussions will stick to the questions raised by the stories themselves and not get guided, uncomfortably, down other paths. Because if we weigh the stories down with the baggage of unrelated lessons, they will sink and disappear. And then there will be a lot of lamentation in the children's book section of that echoing library up in heaven where, I like to imagine, Lewis Carroll and J. M. Barrie and E. B. White and Beatrix Potter and Arnold Lobel and Arthur Rackham and Margot Zemach and all the others who have added so much to our lives meet every morning for milk and cookies and have a good time talking shop.

A good story is sufficient unto the day. It is complete as it stands. If it has something to teach, let it teach in its own sufficiency. Let it keep its magic and fulfill its purpose. In other words, let it be.

Editor Michael di Capua of Farrar, Straus and Giroux, 1966. The author kept this framed photo on her writing desk.

" *We are craftsmen. We labor and sweat. Almost nothing comes easily. And we're something else, too: We're crazy. We're crazy because nobody asks us to go through all that agony. We just do it to satisfy some obscure impulse that refuses to be denied.* "

Beacons of Light

(*1993*)

It is always unsettling to me to hear what we storytellers and picture makers do described as "radiant" or "enlightening." It seems to me that what we really do is more like crawling through a dark and very long tunnel toward that proverbial light glimmering at the end. It may be that at the very beginning of the creative process, once in a while, there is kind of a flash of light, which is one way to describe the sensation of being grabbed by a good initial idea. But the initial idea is such a tiny piece of the whole effort that by the time a book is finished, that particular flash of light has long since been overwhelmed. And if what we've managed to produce can ever be called enlightening or radiant, I think that's got to be more of a fluke than anything else. In any case, one man's radiance is another man's fog. Or so it has seemed in my experience.

Let us remember that while radiance may, in rare instances, describe a book, it never describes the book's creator. We're rather a motley crew, we makers of stories and pictures. We come in all shapes, colors, and sizes, from all regions of the country, and we have next to nothing in common with each other except our product. Some of us are pleasant; some are crabby. Some talk easily; some are silent as the tomb. Some make a lot of money; some barely survive. Some of us look like stereotypical artists with long hair, sandals, and a tortured expression, while some of us, like me, only look like someone's grandmother. It would be nice, I suppose, if we were marked in some way, if we looked radiant and enlightening, but we'd have to *be* radiant and enlightening to begin with in order for that to happen. And we're simply not.

In that magnificent movie *Amadeus*, Mozart's envious colleague, Salieri, is outraged to find Mozart's genius housed in what he calls "a boastful, lustful, smutty, infantile boy." In describing his first encounter with Mozart to a young priest who has come to see him in the insane asylum, Salieri says, "That was Mozart. That giggling, dirty-minded creature I'd just seen crawling on the floor! Why would God choose an obscene child to be his instrument?"

Well, Mozart, who was indeed a genius, is one thing, of course, and we are another thing altogether. I certainly don't want to put any of us in the same class. But Salieri's point is well taken: The creator is neither radiant nor enlightening.

And yet once we are out in the world, away from the

isolation of our work space, we are sometimes treated as if we were radiant and enlightening, and that's very bad for us. It makes for a particularly debilitating form of schizophrenia. Because we do have this one thing in common: We are very uncertain people, with about the same degree of self-confidence as a rabbit on the highway at rush hour.

I have never understood why teachers and librarians are so kind to us, why they set us up so high. The fact is that our careers are utterly and completely in their very capable hands, to be made or destroyed on the pages of a review journal or in the classroom. I refer you briefly to accounts by Sir James George Frazer in his famous work *The Golden Bough*, where he discusses the killing of sacred animals. He talks about a people called the Ainu, on the Japanese island of Yezo, who worshipped the bear as their "chief divinity." The bear, according to Frazer, received "idolatrous veneration" from the Ainu. But when the time came around, they sacrificed the bear, after first apologizing to it, because, says Frazer, they had "treated the bear kindly as long as they could." So much for idolatrous veneration! This is a drastic comparison, I know, but it behooves us to remember, always, who's really in charge here.

If, as I have suggested, storytellers and picture makers are fundamentally unselfconfident, many have learned to hide that fact. Many seem to take themselves with enormous seriousness, so that it's not always easy to see through the sheltering layer of arrogance down to the quaking vulnerability beneath. Well, everybody is to some degree an egotist, regardless of profession. It almost seems as if we are all kept afloat on the sea of life by inner tubes of vanity—the only other choice being to push off in nothing but a sieve of humility and very soon sink completely out of sight. Inner tubes make a pretty good metaphor for the human ego; they are easily deflated and just as easily patched and reinflated. And maybe, if it's true that storytellers and picture makers are especially vulnerable, they need bigger inner tubes just to keep their heads above water.

But we are still nothing but rabbits, and we are not at all radiant. Nevertheless, many of us do take ourselves pretty seriously, especially if we've recently been exposed to "idolatrous veneration" like the Ainu's sacred bear. I wish there were a lot more humor in the field. Humor helps to keep things in balance. When I was in high school, I had a truly fine studio-art teacher who used to take us, from time to time, down to the art museum in Cleveland to study paintings firsthand. And I can remember being irritated, once in a while, at the utter lack of humor and objectivity displayed in some of the paintings we looked at. I always wondered what the artists were like who created those pictures. I guessed they were as humorless and stiff-minded as their work. Janet Moore, my teacher, would tell us that a certain painting was a masterpiece, and I would want to know why. How could a painting be called a masterpiece when it was so smug and self-satisfied? Surely more was required of a masterpiece than perfection of brushwork! We had some good debates, Miss Moore and I. (Years later, she won praise as the author of a fine book about art called *The Many Ways of Seeing*.) She was the soul of patience, given the annoying snip of a teenage heretic I must have been. But the thing is, you could take a smug, self-satisfied painting such as Raphael's portrait of Pope Leo X with the cardinals in the background—a miraculous painting indeed, but very pleased with itself—and you could put into the foreground a large dog, with an expression of utter seriousness on its face, every bit equal to that of the pope and cardinals, except that the dog would be wearing a funny hat. Instantly the painting would acquire another dimension—it would have truth; it would have humanity; it would become accessible—all without losing one iota of its astonishingly beautiful brushwork. Now, that would be a painting! And I, for one, would have liked Signore Raphael personally all the better for it. Still, perhaps Raphael was as uncertain of himself as the rest of us, in spite of his genius, and was only trying to cover up. We'll never know.

The point I'm trying to make is that storytellers and picture makers had better not get themselves confused with their product. We'd better not believe that we ourselves are some kind of beacon to readers. If something we have created somehow becomes a beacon, then we'd better remember it didn't do that all by itself. It had a whole lot of help from teachers and librarians. It would not, in fact, have attracted even a dim-witted night moth, let alone a bright fifth grader, if someone hadn't held it up to be seen. People say a lot of nice things to me about *Tuck Everlasting*, and I'm grateful for every word, but the fact is that I know perfectly well, from the letters I get from the children themselves, that very few of them would ever get past chapter 2 without a gentle but firm push from their teachers.

So here's where I stand on all this: Pictures and stories can be wonderful, and life would be very dreary without them. We are lucky to be living at a moment in time when there is a great accumulated wealth of good books for our children. But so great is the accumulated wealth that, finally, those of us who are making the new stories and the new pictures don't matter. I will repeat that: We don't matter. Childhood is brief—so achingly brief—and there isn't nearly enough time for the children to get around to what's already there for them to look at and to read. If there were no new pictures and stories for the next fifty years, children would feel no lack at all. Think about it. *Alice's Adventures in Wonderland* is still going strong after 128 years; *Treasure Island* after 110. *The Wind in the Willows* is eighty-five years old; *Winnie-the-Pooh* is sixty-seven; *Millions of Cats* is sixty-five; and *Mary Poppins* is fifty-nine. Even *Charlotte's Web*, which somehow seems new, is forty-one years old this year, and *Where the Wild Things Are* is thirty. I'm not saying that we want children to know only the older, proven books, but on the other hand, we don't want them to miss those books, either. So we don't need the four or five thousand new books that make their appearance every year. We simply don't need them.

This being the case, no one should try to make celebrities out of us. We work hard, yes, and sometimes very nice things come out as a result, but we are merely craftsmen who make things nobody really needs. We do it because it's what we *can* do, and what we do best—what we want to do whether the need is there or not. We have, I suppose, what could be called active imaginations, but an active imagination is not always a blessing, and by no means does it always ensure a worthwhile piece of work. My active imagination is much more apt to furnish me with doomsday visions of highway driving than a good idea for a story.

Perhaps those not directly involved in the bookmaking part of our field have a romanticized view of what our working lives are like. Perhaps they envision a light-filled studio where the

Muses hover and where, like magic, we touch a sheet of paper with a paint-filled brush, or tap out a word with a typewriter or computer, and what emerges is something made with joy and ready to be received with joy by a hungry public. But in reality the process is absolutely nothing like that. We are craftsmen. And what that means is that we start with what seems like a good idea—which may have come to us in a flash of light but is far more likely to have emerged after weeks or months of being pushed, pulled, stretched, squashed, laundered, dyed, thrown out, retrieved, reshaped, and finally settled—and then the work begins. The work is hard and long and painstaking. Our legs go to sleep, at least mine do; we bash our heads against the wall; we drudge. And little by little the work gets done.

I have just recently finished a new picture book, after nearly four years. In order to get the pictures to look even remotely like what I saw in my head, I had to make costumes and then plead with my family and my dog to get into them and pose for me while I took hundreds of pictures. I had to find somebody who played the lute so I could see what one really looked like, and how the hands went when they were playing it. I had to comb through dozens of books to find the proper historical settings and props. Then I had to paint the pictures, learning as I went along. When I began, my grandson, who is a prominent character, was one and a half years old. He insisted on getting older all the time, till at last his costume didn't fit him at all and I had to use his little sister instead.

Friends would ask, "How's it coming?" and I would groan and say, "The problem is, I don't know what I'm doing." And they would turn their eyes up to heaven and say, "Yeah—sure!"

But it was true. It's always true, especially if we're always trying to break ground that is new to us. I read somewhere that Maurice Sendak spent weeks testing dozens of different tools before he settled on the ones he used for *In the Night Kitchen*. It's no simple matter, going out to the art store to buy a paintbrush or a pen, to choose just the right kind of paper. And half of what we do has to be done over again, sometimes many times. My picture book has twelve full-page pictures in it, plus a frontispiece and a jacket. Each one took at least six weeks to complete, which doesn't count the costume making and the picture taking, and then the first three had to be done over again because, by the time I got to the twelfth, I knew better how to do what I was trying to do, so that the first three looked inexcusably inept. So—we are craftsmen. We labor and sweat. Almost nothing comes easily. And we're something else, too: We're crazy. We're crazy because nobody asks us to go through all that agony. We just do it to satisfy some obscure impulse that refuses to be denied.

We're craftsmen, we're crazy, and—we are expendable. I said that once to a prominent colleague, and he was so shocked that his mouth dropped open. But it's true. We are expendable. It makes no sense to see us as celebrities. The people who deserve celebrity, the true bringers of light, are the very ones who never get any: the teachers and librarians. Over and over they take a back seat to everyone else. They take a back seat to us crazy people where books are concerned, and what is even more annoying, they take a back seat to their colleagues, the college professors. College professors are held in high esteem in the world. After all, they have PhDs, and they write long books and articles on difficult subjects, and they understand things no one else can make head or tail of. Right? Well, I say phooey. I have spent all of my adult life in the academic world because my husband is a college administrator. Most of my friends are college teachers, and I know that they work very hard and that they aren't well paid compared to people in other professions. But they don't work any harder than elementary-school teachers do, and their salaries, by comparison, are downright princely. And anyway, college professors wouldn't have anyone to teach if it weren't for the elementary schools. And furthermore, I know firsthand from my frequent school visits that the dedication of elementary-school teachers and librarians is unmatched anywhere. It is embarrassing to me, a crazy person who has just spent two whole days painting a picture of a birdcage, to be lionized by one of these amazing people. The injustice of a system which creates this kind of upside-down reasoning makes me angry. I am dispensable. But without *them* the nation's culture would collapse. It's probably not true that the meek shall inherit the earth—and maybe, seeing the shape the earth is in, the meek wouldn't want it anyhow—but I wish with all my heart that things could be ordered differently, and that credit could be given, with a lavish hand, where credit is due.

I also hope we won't forget the reason for all these labors. I hope we won't forget the children. I don't know whether I'm simply getting sentimental as I approach my dotage, but more and more frequently, when I come away from school visits, I find I am moved very near to tears by the children I've just been talking to. They are nearly always fifth graders—my choice—and they seem to me unfailingly wise and calm and beautiful. I am always struck first off by how beautiful they are. I've gone back to my old scrapbook again and again to look at my fifth-grade class picture, and I always find that we were not beautiful, my friends and I. We were scrawny and pasty-faced, and our clothes didn't fit very well. Maybe we were wise and calm—I don't know about that—but we were not beautiful. Well—Janie Dorner was beautiful, of course, but every class since the beginning of time has had a Janie Dorner in it, so she doesn't count.

But today's fifth graders are beautiful. They sit there and look at me skeptically as I come in. They've been told, you see, that I'm a famous author and they should be grateful I'm there. Well, their faces say as I look back at them, they'll be the judge of whether to be grateful or not. I don't look famous. Pretty soon, after I've been there a few minutes, they relax. I'm only a person who makes stories and pictures. They do that, too. The skepticism disappears, and soon we are just talking to each other. They are open, honest, and direct. They laugh easily, but they are not silly. We talk about the Loch Ness monster, about magic water and what an ancient idea that is, about why movies are so often terrible, about pets, theirs and mine—a whole wide range of things. They tell me how boring and confusing the beginning of *Tuck Everlasting* is, and then we talk about what time might look like if you could draw a picture of it. They are wonderful. I know, watching them and listening to them, that in a matter of months they won't be wise and calm anymore, or even half so beautiful. They will turn into hormone machines, as we all did in our turn, and for a few years they will forget how to be open and direct. But for now they are full of imagination; they are radiant; they are luminous; they enlighten. They are, themselves, beacons. They don't know these things about themselves, so I try to tell them. But once again they look skeptical. If the magic water were real, they tell me, they wouldn't drink it now. They wouldn't want to be ten years old forever. Well, of course not. But I'm lucky. I can, and do, go back to the same classrooms year after year, and they are always full to the brim with the same enduring light.

So this is the light that matters. This is why we do the work we do, all of us. We will go on doing it the very best we can, whether we are the necessary ones or only the crazy, expendable ones. I only hope that we, the writers and illustrators, will stop congratulating ourselves, for the miracle doesn't reside in us at all. I don't want to put down what I and my immediate colleagues do. There are always genuine moments of inspiration, and of those we can all stand in awe. It's just that I think the makers of stories and pictures have been in the limelight too long. There are a lot of very good writers and illustrators working hard in our field, and what they do is important, but the part that's important is not our own books and art. It is the gift of a love of books and art in general. The gift won't be accepted by all children, not even by a majority. But if a child learns to love books and art while he's in elementary school, chances are he'll love them all his life. And oh, what a privilege that is! To know you have helped to pre-pare the way for Charles Dickens, for Herman Melville, for Jane Austen, for any of the great writers for adults. And for all the painters from Michelangelo to Georgia O'Keeffe. But, you see, the people who make the stories and pictures for children are only a small part of the number laboring toward that end. We have the publicity departments behind us, we get the prizes, we get all the attention; but that is misleading and unjustified.

My fifth-grade teacher's name was Mrs. Wilson. I have remembered her with love for fifty years: what she looked like, how she sounded, what she did for me. But except for the children's classics that were read aloud to me, I remember very few of the books I took home from the library every week, or the names of their authors and illustrators. All I remember is how much fun it was to go to the library and take out the books and read them.

Acts of light were performed every day by Mrs. Wilson and my librarian. We take those acts of light for granted, like the daily rising of the sun. But this is a mistake. We should never take them for granted because without them we couldn't see to read. There is a disagreeable old saying that goes, "Those who can, do. Those who can't, teach." I would like to correct that old saying, which is long overdue for a rewrite. Let it read: "Those who can, teach. Those who can't, be grateful for those who can."

Illustration from *Kneeknock Rise*, winner of a Newbery Honor in 1971

" *Writing about the characters we choose can be a way of re-designing ourselves, if only in our imaginations.* "

Finding Paths

(*1999*)

I 've been thinking about what it might mean to be a pathfinder. And after a lot of pondering, I've come to the conclusion that I myself seem to have tried as hard as I could *not* to find any paths. What I've done is try—though without much success—to cling to paths I already have. But the characters in my stories do seem to seek out new paths. Or maybe they don't; maybe it only looks as if they did. It's time to try to make some sense of this by comparing my own experiences with theirs.

The world I grew up in was very different from the world as it is today. The year I was born, 1932, was a uniquely scary time.

The economy had fallen apart completely, and hundreds of thousands of people, including my father, lost their jobs. Some of them lost their hopes, too, and jumped off bridges or out the windows of tall buildings. My father didn't do that, thank goodness. He had too strong a sense of humor. But my family, which consisted pretty much only of my parents, my older sister, and me, did do something that I can only suppose was a common thing to do at the time: We drew together into a tight little unit and took a stand, us against the world. My father assumed that everything would eventually be all right.

My mother, who was as strong and determined as a corporate CEO, didn't assume anything; instead, she reached out to protect us all. My sister has said since that when she was little she used to think of our mother as a stone wall with two blue marbles in it, the marbles, of course, being our mother's eyes.

In the thirties, I was too little to know exactly what was going on. And I wasn't told, either. But at all ages you sense things. Even as a preschooler, I sensed danger in the world. If you know you're being protected, you're naturally going to assume that there's something out there to be protected *from*. At least, that's what I assumed. So I wasn't quite as genuinely defiant as my more sensible sister. I could pretend a pretty good defiance if my mother was there to back me up, but I wasn't very good at it otherwise. And my mother, who liked being in control anyway, was happy to have me stay dependent on her.

Near the beginning of *Tuck Everlasting*, Winnie Foster thinks about running away, but soon decides against it. Here are a few lines from that part:

"Where would I go, anyway?" she asked herself. "There's nowhere else I really want to be." But in another part of her head, the dark part where her oldest fears were housed, she knew there was another sort of reason for staying at home: she was afraid to go away alone.

It was one thing to talk about being by yourself, doing important things, but quite another when the opportunity arose. The characters in the stories she read always seemed to go off without a thought or care, but in real life—well, the world was a dangerous place. People were always telling her so. And she would not be able to manage without protection. They were always telling her that, too. No one ever said precisely what it was that she would not be able to manage. But she did not need to ask. Her own imagination supplied the horrors.

When I go to schools to talk to the kids who've been reading my stories, they often ask where my characters come from, and I tell them that all main characters tend to be like the person who wrote the story, because the main character's eyes are the eyes through which the events of the story are seen. I tell them that Winnie Foster is a lot like me. But I add that she's braver than I am, and the example I give is that I've never picked up a toad and don't intend to start now. They think that's funny, and of course it is, in its way. Also, it's true. I never *have* picked up a toad. However, Winnie Foster is braver than I am in ways that are much more important than that. Winnie is afraid in the beginning, but in the first of the short few days that the story takes to spin itself out, she tries to defy that fear, and takes the first steps toward overcoming it when she goes into the wood early the next morning.

But I would never have gone into the wood. I would have stayed home where it was safe. Life forces us sometimes to take risks, but the risks taken by the person who doesn't want to take them are very different from the risks taken by a pathfinder.

I could whine that my fearfulness was and is all my mother's fault, my mother and the Depression. But my sister was never full of fears, even with the same mother. And as for the Depression, well, I have a friend who lives in New Orleans who is exactly the same age I am, so she went through the Depression, too. Many parts of her life and her reactions to them are exactly like mine. We are both from small towns in the Midwest, our husbands have many things in common, and so do our children and our dogs. We are a lot alike. But a few years ago, Joan decided it was time to wrench herself away from her very demanding family for a couple of weeks. She signed up to be an aide in a research program on orangutans, and went gaily off to Borneo without a backward look. The only thing she was worried about was snakes. There are a lot of snakes in Borneo. But she went anyway.

Nothing—*nothing*—could get me to go to Borneo. I don't even want to go to Akron. This is not because of snakes or automobile tires. It is because, like Winnie Foster at the beginning of her story, I am afraid to go away alone. I often have gone away alone, on gigs having to do with children's books, to remote places all around this country, from northernmost Montana to central Arkansas, and from seacoast California to seacoast Florida. I did it because I was told that I had to. But I never got over being afraid: not of the gig itself, but of being far from home and alone.

Thinking about this in connection with pathfinding has made me wonder, though, about the motivations of writers. An idea for a story comes out of nowhere and presents itself to the front of your brain, and you get excited about it, and then you settle back and become a craftsman, and work out the plot and the casting of characters, and proceed to tell the story the very best way you can. Nobody has to remind you that something has to happen in a story, that a problem has to be there for the hero to face and solve. At least, in a story for children the problem has to be solved. You will long since have learned to be objective about what you're doing. You don't go breathlessly along in some kind of haze of love for the initial idea and your cleverness in having thought of it. So most of the time you don't search out the origins of that initial idea. What does it matter where it came from? Well, actually, it *doesn't* matter where it came from. But you see, I have a son who's a psychologist, and—well, let me back up just a bit. You may not be familiar with a little picture book of mine called *Nellie: A Cat on Her Own*. The jacket flap, which I had to write myself, says:

Nellie is a marionette, but she is also a cat—a cat marionette who loves to dance. When she is left on her own by the clever old woman who made her, she believes that her dancing is over forever, but her friend,

Big Tom—a real cat, with fur—takes her away with him to a moonlit hilltop where there is a gathering of friends. What happens then may be moonshine or magic, or possibly both.

This appears to be a pretty simple story. I didn't think much about where the idea came from; it didn't seem to matter. But I sent a copy to my son, who usually keeps his analyzing at a healthy distance from the family. This time, however, when he called me to thank me for the book, he said, "Mom, you know—there's a whole lot going on here." So I went back and looked at the story again from his perspective, and was naïve enough to be astonished. Well, gee whiz! *Nellie* is, in fact, a mini-autobiography! A mini-autobiography with an idealized ending, yes, but a mini-autobiography just the same.

I've talked about this with writing colleagues and they all confess to discovering the same kind of thing in their own stories. It comes as no surprise to anyone but us, of course. Everyone except the writer knows that any piece of fiction is going to be full of the psyche of the person who wrote it. But the point is not that I wrote a story about a character who is left alone in a dangerous world. The point is that the character takes charge as well as she can, makes a choice, and builds a life from the available ingredients. In other words, stories can move beyond autobiography into a kind of therapy. Writing about the characters we choose can be a way of redesigning ourselves, if only in our imaginations. Because, you see, if I had really been Nellie, taken away to dance in the moonlight by the real cat, Big Tom, I would have enjoyed it as long as I could dance with him, but the next day, no way would I have stayed behind in a hollow tree the way Nellie does. I would have taken Big Tom up on his offer to find me a new old woman to take care of me. And what kind of a story would *that* have made of it? Not too satisfying.

And yet, pathfinders come in a lot of different shapes and sizes. In *The Wizard of Oz*, Dorothy is never a coward. She faces up to trial after trial. But first and foremost, she is always trying to find a way to go home to Kansas. In other words, she may be finding paths she wouldn't necessarily have chosen to find. However, the going home is an important ingredient of the path of the classic hero: You have to go home at the end of your adventures. I doubt that L. Frank Baum knew anything on a conscious level about the path of the classic hero, but Joseph Campbell, in his *Hero with a Thousand Faces*, claims that we all know the pattern subconsciously.

But it's a *pattern*. It doesn't necessarily mirror real life. Let me tell you a little about my ancestors, the ones from whom my father's mother was descended. Their name was Zane, and they came over here from England before the Revolution. They hurried out to the frontier, which was then more or less in Ohio, and literally made a path which was afterward called Zane's Trace, a path that angled down southwest across a piece of Ohio and was used for a while by other pioneers. And then they fought in the Revolution. And then—and then—nothing! No more paths. The frontier moved on past Ohio, ever westward; new pioneers hurried by on Lake Erie or on the Ohio River. But the Zanes stayed where they were and did nothing of interest ever again, and this definitely includes my father's mother. Ohio itself isn't interesting anymore. Hasn't been interesting for a couple of centuries.

I sometimes feel that my ancestors bear some part of the blame for that fact, but it's too late now to do anything about it.

Anyway, the point I'm trying to make is that there is nothing in my life that bears any resemblance to the finding of paths, either literally or figuratively. On the contrary. So how has this fact influenced the stories I've written? I guess my stories are, at bottom, not built around adventures at all, but rather around ideas. Well, I don't guess; I know. Ideas are the real protagonists. Nice, comfortable ideas you can carry around without leaving the house. Things happen to my characters because there's no story if nothing happens, but they all go home afterward and never leave again. Winnie Foster in *Tuck Everlasting* spends the rest of her life in Treegap and is buried there. Just like the Zanes and Ohio. Hercules Feltwright in *Goody Hall* goes home to Hackston Fen at the end. In *Kneeknock Rise*, Ada and her family will stay in Instep. Why not? They like it there. Even a cousin like Egan can't destroy their pleasure in their monster. In *The Eyes of the Amaryllis*, an irritating visitor says to Jenny's grandmother, "However have you kept yourself amused in this boring old place?" To which Gran replies, "Why should I leave? This is my home." And in *The Search for Delicious*, Gaylen settles down to being mayor of the first town and marries a hometown girl. The minstrel in that story is the only wanderer I've ever cast as a character. But I think you feel a little sorry for him somehow, poor homeless nomad. I wrote *Delicious* in the late sixties, which is not unimportant to the kind of story it is. The minstrel is like many young people in those days, tramping around with guitars, trying to make peace while the world made war.

So my characters have had their adventures, yes, but they've always gone home afterward. And it has been the going home I've envied them, not their adventures. I've moved twenty-nine times, finding new homes on the average once every two and a half years, sometimes down the street and sometimes in a whole new state. That's what a lot of us do here in America. We move. Nothing unusual about it. I'm different, if at all, only in the fact that the paths I've trodden, I've mostly trodden kicking and screaming.

It's possible, of course, that pathfinding means something else. I've seen pathfinders described as precursors, pavers of the way who open doors for themselves and others. But you can't pave ways and open doors without leaving home, or so it seems to me. Leaving home not only physically, but philosophically, too. Is it possible to stay at home physically while you're leaving philosophically? I'm not sure about that. If it is possible, maybe it's one of the many reasons why people write stories in the first place.

But I'm not sure about that, either. People like the Brontë sisters seem to have written stories to open up the constrictions of their world. Harriet Beecher Stowe wanted to change society. Some writers want to make money and got the idea from somewhere that writing is easy and will make you rich and famous. Agatha Christie said she wrote to support herself after her husband died. Beatrix Potter stopped writing after she got married. Some seem to write because they enjoy suffering; Leo Tolstoy is reported by his wife to have been so frustrated sometimes with the composition of *War and Peace* that he literally rolled on the floor and wailed.

I think that on the whole I prefer to believe you can divide all people, writers included, into two groups: those who find paths and those who stay home. Kenneth Grahame understood about this. I think he and I would have gotten along very well, at least on the question of pathfinders and stay-at-homes. There's a beautiful chapter in *The Wind in the Willows* entitled "Wayfarers All," in which the Rat, sitting beside the river, is joined by another rat, a dusty one, says Grahame, who salutes "with a gesture of courtesy" that has "something foreign about it." This wayfarer turns out to be a self-described seafaring rat whose preferred habitat is in the captain's cabins of ships in the coasting trade. He is a hugely articulate wayfarer who woos the imagination of Ratty with long, rich descriptions of days and nights on the water, and days and nights in foreign ports. Italy, Sicily, Sardinia, Corsica, all are familiar to him, and so are Lisbon, Oporto, and Bordeaux, Cornwall and Devon, and the seacoast towns of Spain. "Spell-bound and quivering with excitement," Grahame tells us,

> the Water Rat followed the Adventurer league by league, over stormy bays, through crowded roadsteads, across harbour bars on a racing tide, up winding rivers that hid their busy little towns round a sudden turn . . . [And so] the wonderful talk flowed on—or was it speech entirely or did it pass at times into song—chanty of the sailors weighing the dripping anchor, sonorous hum of the shrouds in a tearing North-Easter, ballad of the fisherman hauling his nets at sundown against an apricot sky, chords of guitar and mandoline from gondola or caique?

The talk puts Ratty—and the reader, too—into a dreaming state with its beauty, till at last the wayfarer leaves him with these words:

> *And you, you will come, too, young brother; for the*
> *days pass, and never return, and the South still waits*
> *for you. Take the Adventure, heed the call, now ere*
> *the irrevocable moment passes! 'Tis but a banging of*
> *the door behind you, a blithesome step forward, and*
> *you are out of the old life and into the new! . . . You*
> *can easily overtake me on the road, for you are young,*
> *and I am ageing and go softly. I will linger, and look*
> *back; and at last I will surely see you coming, eager*
> *and light-hearted, with all the South in your face!*

And with this the seafaring rat disappears down the road.

Ratty stumbles home, still half hypnotized, and begins to pack his necessary belongings—moving, says Grahame, like a sleepwalker. This alarms his housemate, the Mole, who grapples with him, forcing him down, and the Rat at last lies trembling, exhausted, and begins to weep. Mole is anxious about him but leaves him alone, trying to bring life around him back to normal, and at last Ratty, still shaken but acknowledging to himself that his fit has passed, begins to sit up and join in. Grahame ends the chapter this way:

> *Presently the tactful Mole slipped away and returned*
> *with a pencil and a few half-sheets of paper, which*
> *he placed on the table at his friend's elbow.*

"It's quite a long time since you did any poetry,"
he remarked. "You might have a try at it this evening,
instead of—well, brooding over things so much. I've
an idea that you'll feel a lot better when you've got
something jotted down—if it's only just the rhymes."

The Rat pushed the paper away from him wea-
rily, but the discreet Mole took occasion to leave
the room, and when he peeped in again some time
later, the Rat was absorbed and deaf to the world;
alternately scribbling and sucking the top of his pen-
cil. It is true that he sucked a good deal more than he
scribbled, but it was joy to the Mole to know that the
cure had at least begun.

The seafaring rat is a true pathfinder, in the terms described a few paragraphs back: He is a paver of the way who tries to open doors for Ratty, and to challenge the boundaries of his thinking. The fact that he is unsuccessful is not a measure of the beauty of his words or his way of telling what wonders might be Ratty's for the asking.

And yet, has he really been unsuccessful? We don't know what Ratty is writing in the above chapter's end, but we can guess. If I may be allowed to speak for us all, Ratty, who is a poet, has begun an epic about a rat who leaves home and everything familiar behind him for a life of marvelous, groundbreaking adventure. And the pleasure he gains from his writing is as real and as thrilling to his imagination as the thing itself would have been.

My characters would have stayed behind, too, though only one was a poet. I admire pathfinders, but though I said at the beginning of this paper that my characters seem to seek out new paths, I think now that when all is said and done, they don't, not really. Not like the seafaring rat of "Wayfarers All." For my characters, each in his or her own story, one adventure will be enough to light up a whole life. Pathfinders will always be welcome in my house. But if they want to go to Borneo, they'll have to go alone.

Book signing, 1998

“*We humans, with our indomitable egos, are equipped with two qualities which . . . have served us well from the beginning and made survival if not possible, then certainly palatable: First, we are blessed with the ability to laugh, and second, we are storytellers.*”

New World, No World

(2001)

Some people think there's a brave new world coming. I am not among them. I think it will only be the same old world wearing a different hat. For a while, anyway. Perhaps this is because I'm getting old, myself. For, in Shakespeare's *The Tempest*, when Miranda says, "O brave new World,/That has such people in't," her father, Prospero, doesn't agree. He merely strokes his white beard and replies, " 'Tis new to thee."

Of course, there are electronic developments coming along fast and furious these days, so that television, for instance, is getting better and better in the way it produces images. The newness won't stop, I suppose, though I'm not sure you could call it brave. But what's the *use* of it? The shows aren't getting better and better. Now and then there is a terrific new one, but then it goes into reruns forever and ever. Not that that's necessarily a bad thing, you know; better a rerun of a good show than a first run of a bad show. Still, it can get a little tiresome. Except when, once in a while, someone puts on a retrospective of a really old series like *Your Show of Shows* with Sid Caesar and Imogene Coca. The sound has no subtlety; the pictures are scratchy, black-and-white, far from easy on the eyes. They could use a few electronic developments. But oh, what wonderful shows they were, and still are, just as they stand!

Movies aren't getting any braver and newer, either, no matter how their screens expand or wrap around or cram themselves together fourteen at a time into one building. Movies are scrambling for new story ideas already, even before the future gets here, and seem forced to go in for remakes, old ideas in new hats. Once in a while something new and delicious does come along—*Shrek*, for instance, though I heard, without surprise, that William Steig has said he thinks it's a funny movie but it's not *his* story. Yes, *Shrek* is genuinely funny, and genuinely new—funny and new for almost all the right reasons—but it's a huge exception. In a recent interview in the *New York Times*, revered *New Yorker* movie critic Pauline Kael complained that a lot of movies nowadays are such immediate blockbusters at the box office that there's no way for a critic to point out how bad they are. "If you say something negative about the big hits," she said, "it's like sour grapes. You can't argue against them; they're beyond criticism."

Email is certainly a brave new convenience, as long as it's controlled—control may be a real factor for the future to deal with—but the letters themselves, written on a computer, aren't any better than the letters that were written on typewriters, which in their turn weren't any better than the letters written by hand, with pens. Words are words, however they're rendered. I was in the main Providence post office the other day, and the stamp clerk told me there was an inside rumor going around that, in the near future, federal post offices would probably be delivering mail only three times a week, now that so many people use email. That was hard to imagine, and sad to imagine. Thank goodness they've apparently decided to let things stand. I've been waiting happily for the mail every day since 1937 when Sonja Henie, in response to the first and only fan letter I ever wrote, sent me an autographed picture. If you don't know who Sonja Henie was, well, too bad for you. Anyway, the mail has magic for me. True, that letter with the check for five million dollars hasn't appeared yet, but as long as there's a mailman, there's hope, isn't there? Somehow, the news that you've become a multimillionaire would seem a lot less reliable if you got it on a computer screen than it would inside an envelope. But maybe that's only my opinion. You who have grown up with computers probably wouldn't agree.

As for books, Roger Sutton said it all in his most recent elegant, well-reasoned, and gratifying *Horn Book* editorial. When a magazine reporter called him for his reaction to news that a publisher was planning to continue C. S. Lewis's Chronicles of Narnia with books commissioned from other writers, his first thought was to scorn anyone involved in such a project. But then, he says, "I stopped fretting about my display of critical invective and started instead to worry about what this kind of cloning-by-corporation means for children's books." Talk about your reruns and remakes and sequels! There are a lot of timid souls these days in some of the publishing houses, if it's possible to be, at one and the same time, timid and venal. They're timid about taking chances on new writers with new ideas, because these might not make any money. *Harry Potter* has been a blessing for kids, but it's been rather a disaster for the field in general. It demonstrates too graphically that there's real money to be had out there, if only you can find the formula. But, well, I suppose that's not so new a condition, either, when you come right down to it. Finding the formula is the same thing as striking oil, or hitting on the vein of gold. We like that kind of thing here in America. We like making money. Sudden, big money. It's mainly why our ancestors came over here in the first place: riches, the land that contained them, and the freedom to go out and look for them. And there's no reason to think the idea will lose its grip on us in the future.

It's true that a lot of things about the modern world are different from what they used to be, and these same things will be even more different fifty years from now, five hundred years from now. But allow me to stress that it's *things* that are different. People aren't any different, and it's people who count, people who embody the real essence of life. We're still made up of all the contradictory things that have always defined us, and we aren't any better or any worse than we ever were. We just seem that way from time to time. And by "us" I mean children as well as adults. Are children any different from what they always were? Well, judge for yourselves. Here's a quote I came across a few weeks ago in an airplane magazine: "Children today are tyrants. They contradict their parents, gobble their food, and tyrannize their teachers." The person who said this clearly thought children were worse than they used to be. But would you care to guess *who* said it, and *when*? Don't bother; I'll tell you. Socrates said it, and he said it sometime around 440 BC, in the neighborhood of two and a half thousand years ago. So if children aren't any worse or any better than they always were, if people in general aren't any worse or any better than they always were, what then? What is the meaning of a brave new world?

Maybe this new frontier we're told is coming isn't going to be all that new. Maybe the changes are only going to be superficial. And yet, who can be sure? I wish I could be sure. But I'm no historian, no sociologist, not any kind of scientist, neither a seer nor a fortune-teller. And the funny thing is that as a person gets older, the future holds less and less interest. The introductory phrase "fifty years from now," which had so much clout for my generation fifty years ago, now only brings on a shrug. *We* don't care. We won't *be* here. Except there are aspects of the time fifty years from now that we do care about. The environment, for instance. The education of our great-grandchildren. Little things like that.

But aside from those few details, the only part of the future that interests me is so far in the future that it scarcely qualifies as something to care about, and yet it's been hanging around in my mind since I first learned about the solar system. It's been hanging around in my mind, and it's been shaping the way I look at a great many things, not just the night sky. I always say, when asked where my ideas come from, that they seem to have come out of questions that have been with me since I was a preschooler, questions that don't have any answers, or at least no easy ones. The one I'm referring to now has never turned up in one of my stories, but it's only waiting its turn, and here it is: How can there be nothing out there on the other side of the universe?

When I was in school, I read a lot of Greek and Roman myths, and I read them in a lot of different versions, starting with Hawthorne's *Wonder Book* and *Tanglewood Tales*, and moving on from there to the livelier and more easily read versions in one volume of a set we had that has no name in my memory of it, and was simply called by my sister and me "the blue books." I loved those stories, and read them over and over for years, the whole thing culminating with the publication in 1945 of Robert Graves's *Hercules, My Shipmate*, which is a glorious retelling of the story of Jason and the Argonauts and the search for the golden fleece. Three years after its publication, I was studying Latin in my sophomore year of high school, where we were reading versions of the myths. Well, I was *supposedly* studying and reading Latin. I seem to recall that it was this very Latin teacher, a certain well-named Miss Stoner, who wrote for my midyear report, *Her attitude somewhat lacks seriousness.* However that may have been, I had already read *Hercules, My Shipmate* with immense enthusiasm when Miss Stoner held a copy up in front of our class and acknowledged its scholarship but warned us against its eroticism and told us not to read it. So I went back to the library, checked it out, and read it again.

Now, I'm telling you all this about my relationship with the Greek myths in order to make sure you understand that it was not a scholarly relationship. The myths were great storytelling, is what. The names of their characters were preserved in the constellations, all heavily romantic. And they formed a screen between me and that unanswered question: How can there be nothing on the other side of the universe? Leaving Miss Stoner behind, I went on to college, where there was a science requirement. One of the options was a beginning course in astronomy. "Hey!" I said to myself. "The myths!" I entered the class, mooned about on top of the observatory drawing the constellations in the freezing New England dark, wrote a paper about Jason and Medea, and solidly flunked the midyear exam. An attitude that somewhat lacked seriousness was not an excuse for anything at college. It didn't even provoke a comment from the dean. Sink or swim is the way it went at college. Well, finally I swam, sort of. I managed to pass the course with a C-minus in the spring. And then, whether because of me or not, but probably not—when you're young, you think everything is because of you—the professor resigned her appointment and, so they say, left the college and went to Florida to become a hotel hostess. Life is sometimes every bit as interesting as a Greek myth.

And all that time, the question hung suspended: How can there be nothing on the other side of the universe? What is the meaning of nothing? And if there's really nothing, then what's the meaning of *anything*? My sister, with far more of a scholarly mind than I could lay claim to, told me that in the process of attempting to confront the question herself, she found that all at once she was looking squarely at the outermost limit of her intelligence, the place where it ended, the wall beyond which she simply could not go. This is a good description of the situation. Here we are, considering what the future may be like, and while we consider, out there beyond our walls, beyond the city, beyond this continent, beyond all the world's oceans and mountains, beyond Cassiopeia and the Big Dipper, beyond the sun itself, space goes on and on and on, dark and cold and blank except for the occasional star, without clocks or calendars, without air or water, even without an up or a down. So what do we make of that? What *can* we make of that, given the limits of human intelligence?

Well, some human intelligences are less limited than others. The June 25 issue of *Time* magazine soberly announces, on its cover, a feature article about "How the Universe Will End" with this for a teaser: "Peering deep into space and time, scientists have just solved the biggest mystery in the cosmos." The article is wonderful, fascinating, utterly humbling. It says that for a long time there have been two conflicting theories about how things will come to a finish: One is that the momentum caused by the big bang will turn around and bring everything hurtling back again into itself, causing what they call a big crunch, and the other is that the big-bang momentum will keep on sending things outward forever. Now scientists have proved to their satisfaction—please don't ask me how—that the second theory is correct: The world will end as T. S. Eliot said it would, "not with a bang but a whimper." "Earth should remain habitable for another few billion years," says the article, and then, in what it calls a degenerate era, lasting trillions of years, planets, and here I more or less quote, will "detach from stars; stars and planets evaporate from galaxies. Most of the ordinary matter in the universe [will be] locked up in degenerate stellar remnants—dead stars that have withered into white dwarfs or blown up and collapsed into neutron stars and black holes. Eventually, over spans of time greatly exceeding the current age of the universe, the protons themselves [will] decay." After this comes a black-hole era lasting more trillions of years than I could grasp, and then—and then comes the dark era, in which there will be virtually nothing at all. "From here into the infinite future," says the article, "the universe remains cold, dark and dismal." And, it suggests, "that will be that—unless, of course, whatever inconceivable event that launched the original Big Bang should recur, and the ultimate free lunch is served once more." This, however, would appear to be entirely unlikely, at least scientifically, although you could look at it biblically and draw the conclusion that, since we seem to be messing things up this time around, the way we did before the Flood, the gods are going to wipe the slate clean and have one more fresh try at the whole experiment.

However that may be, consider the sentence "Earth should remain habitable for another few billion years." Is it a relief to know that we don't have to sell everything just yet and get out the cloaks and robes? It's really too soon to go up to a mountaintop to wait for the end, the way some sects keep doing. And after all, why should we care anyway? We won't be here. It will be as Prospero predicts in Shakespeare's *Tempest*, when he says:

> *The cloud-capp'd towers, the gorgeous palaces,*
> *The solemn temples, the great globe itself,*
> *Yea, all which it inherit, shall dissolve*
> *And, like this insubstantial pageant faded,*
> *Leave not a rack behind.*

But even if we don't care, since this future I've been talking about is such a long way off, even so, all this new information will still hang around in the backs of our minds. How will we deal with the concept of an approaching degenerate era, followed by a black-hole era, and then followed by nothing at all, a great big zero?

Well, what I think is that we will deal with it the way we've always dealt with it. The concept of an end to the world is not, after all, a new concept. It wasn't even new in Shakespeare's day. It is tied inescapably to the concept of our own deaths, and so goes back to the very beginning. Likewise, the concept of there being nothing on the other side of the universe isn't new, either, whether the intelligence of most of us can grasp it or not. I think it will go right on being impossible to look out at the night sky and not wonder what's out there beyond the Milky Way, as long as there's a Milky Way to wonder about. For some of the more adventuresome of us, it's impossible not to push the science as far as it will go so that we can look, either through an immense telescope or through the window of a spaceship. We want to know, we're scared to know, we peek and shiver, and we even laugh. Remember that lovely story about President Reagan, in a cabinet meeting, suggesting an exploratory trip to the sun? "But, Mr. President," protests a secretary, "we can't do that! It would be far too hot." The president pauses, thinks this over, and finally says triumphantly, "Well, then, we'll go at night!"

As I've already said, the question "What is the meaning of nothing?" is logically followed by another question: "If there's nothing, then what is the meaning of anything?" But this, too, is a very old question which we have always answered by ignoring its implications and continuing to assign meaning to whatever we choose, thereafter fighting to the death anyone who has assigned meaning to something else. Or if not fighting, then at least cling-ing comfortably to routine. Someone is supposed to have asked Saint Francis of Assisi once what he would do if he knew the world was coming to an end, and he is supposed to have answered that he'd go right on hoeing his garden. So maybe we're all crazy. I don't know. But we have our good points. It seems to me that, random though our development may have been, however poorly we may run our various societies, however cruel and self-serving and greedy we may be, and however disinterested nature may be in our welfare, we humans, with our indomitable egos, are equipped with two qualities which will serve us well as things progress, which have served us well from the beginning and made survival if not possible, then certainly palatable: First, we are blessed with the ability to laugh, and second, we are storytellers.

There's no way to know for certain what the stories we tell will be like as the future hurries by, but stories will happen. They always have. We will be telling them until close to the end of those few billion years that the Earth has left. They will be the same stories we've always told: stories about our world, our fears, our dreams, the things that make us laugh. They will be stories that will give us ways to imagine, understand, and deal with all the mysteries of our lives, from thunderstorms to black holes in the universe, just as they've always done. And when those few bil-lion years are all used up, well, who cares what happens then? There won't be anybody left to wonder.

I don't think it matters much *how* these future stories will be told. Probably they will be like the letters I mentioned in the be-ginning: just the same whether sent by email, or typed, or writ-ten out longhand with a pen. Or performed by an elder sitting near the campfire. Or scratched wordless onto the walls of a cave. Maybe what we know physically as books won't survive, but so what? The important thing is that the stories keep coming, not what form they will take. One thing is for sure: The changes will be taken for granted by the children of their times. What child today is astonished by computers? My generation may be astonished, but they're not. When they are grown, there will be changes that astonish *them*, but *their* children won't turn a hair. And so it will go. Each new batch of changes will seem completely everyday and natural to each new batch of children. The important thing is the stories themselves and the unchanging human nature they serve. A woman named Irene Peter, about whom I know absolutely nothing, is reported to have said, and I quote, "Just because everything is different doesn't mean anything has changed."

So we'll go right on, regardless, doing what we need to do to make life seem worthwhile, and I'm not going to worry about it. I dislike change; however, I never was able to stop it from coming into my life, and won't *ever* be able to stop it. But I am temporary. So are we all. The best thing to do is to look at the night sky once in a while and remember that *everything* is temporary. And then go right on dealing with the human things we all have to deal with. Some of these things can give us immense pleasure and satisfaction, and the comfort of knowing there *are* things that matter, things that have meaning for us and will go right on having meaning through every one of those few billion years life has remaining. Children, for instance. And stories. There are a few things, thank goodness, that won't change at all.

March/April 2000

The Horn
Book
Magazine

About Books for Children and Young Adults

The author's painting of the man in the yellow suit, for
the cover of the *Horn Book Magazine*

" *The fundamental reason why* Alice in Wonderland *was my favorite book
was that it confirmed my long-held suspicion—long held even by fourth
grade—that grown-ups, and the world they have created, are mad.*
"

We're All Mad Here

(2004)

C hildren often ask me to name the book that was my favorite when I was their age, and I always tell them it was
Alice in Wonderland. The real title is *Alice's Adventures in Wonderland*, of course, but nobody calls it that. I don't know why,
except that it takes longer to say, but I guess it doesn't really
matter. In any case, when I tell children about *Alice*, I don't go
into *all* the reasons why it was my favorite. I do say the pictures
were important. It was the pictures that made me decide to become a children's book illustrator when I grew up. I made this
decision when I was in the fourth grade, and I never really changed
my mind. But there was more to it than the pictures, and that's

what I want to talk about tonight. After all, it's spring at last, and what better time to go out on a limb?

The fundamental reason why *Alice in Wonderland* was my favorite book was that it confirmed my long-held suspicion—long held even by fourth grade—that grown-ups, and the world they have created, are mad. For the most part, they operate on systems that have no basis in rationality. Children are rational, but their elders are not, and can't explain anything. (As in the question "Why do I have to do that?" to which the answer is "Because I said so.") Is it possible to reason irrationally? Certainly. The grown-up characters in *Alice* reason irrationally at a great rate all through the book. There is only one rational character in the *Alice* stories, and that character is Alice herself.

I became aware of the madness of adults, and puzzled over it, long before I was familiar with *Alice*. It began when I was a preschooler. In order to demonstrate that, I will have to tell you four brief stories. For those who've heard all my stories before, and there'll be a few of you, I recommend an alphabet game that I often play when there's time to pass. Starting with *A*, try to think of one foreign and four American major cities for each of the twenty-six letters. No fair using some dinky town nobody else has ever heard of. And I promise you I'll be finished with these stories long before you've fought your way through to *M*, let alone *Z*. All right. Back to the fact of the madness of adults.

To the best of my recollection, my awareness of irrationality began when I was four. It began small, but it began memorably. My sister, who is two years older than I am, was at school, and I was alone in the kitchen, sitting on some kind of a high chair, where I'd been told firmly by my mother to stay until I finished my lunch. I'd been there for quite a while, because there were canned pears for dessert, and I was putting off the necessity of dealing with them. I didn't like canned pears. Still don't. Canned pears, unlike fresh ones, have strings in them. My mother knew I didn't like them, but served them to me anyway. Her plea, in such situations, was that I think of the starving Armenians. But since I didn't know who the Armenians were, or why they were starving, my patience was short. On this particular day, it finally ran out. I climbed down from my high chair and threw my pears in the sink. And then I went down the hall toward the front door, passing my mother, who was headed in the other direction. I was stopped with my hand on the doorknob by my mother's voice from the kitchen. She called to me and said, "Whose pears are these in the sink?"

Now, at the age of four, I was probably not familiar with the word *irrational*. Nevertheless, I clearly recall being puzzled by this question from my mother. At that particular moment, she and I were the only ones in the house, with the exception of our bulldog, Big Mike. But Big Mike had a weak stomach and was therefore never given pears to eat, canned or otherwise, and even if he had, it's unlikely he'd have thrown them in the sink. And of course my mother knew *she* hadn't done it. So when she asked whose pears they were, I decided to answer in the same vein, singsonging back from the front door, "I don't know!" And got spanked for it. Well, I'm not sure if I got spanked for saying "I don't know" or if it was because I threw my pears in the sink in spite of the starving Armenians. But that's not the point. The point is, why did my mother ask such an irrational question?

Then there was the time when Mildred, a friend who lived

next door, stole some doll underwear from my sister when the three of us were playing outside. My sister and I both saw her do it. We ran into our house and complained loudly to our mother. But she, feisty as she was about most things, only said in this case that heaven will punish sinners. You know how it goes—and I quote: "Leave her to heaven." For the next few days, full of expectation, I watched the house next door, but nothing at all happened. At last I decided that if heaven didn't care what Mildred did, it wouldn't care what *I* did, either. So, while my sister was at school, I took out her brand-new scooter—which I had expressly been told not to touch—and rode it off down the sidewalk. But I hit a bump, fell over, and bloodied my nose. For a very long time after this, I believed that heaven had put that bump there to punish me. But why punish me and not Mildred? I was just as good as Mildred. Maybe even better. I couldn't make it out.

Two years later, after a move to another town, my sister and I were walking home from the public swimming pool that was only a park away from our house. It was the middle of summer. And all at once, out of the blue, my sister informed me that there wasn't any Santa Claus. At first I thought she was pulling my leg, but it soon became apparent that she was telling the truth. I don't remember whether she and I discussed the situation. What I decidedly do remember is being, first, angry about the deception, and then mystified. It was grown-ups who had made the whole thing up, that much was clear, but why? Yes, the Santa Claus story was jolly, but that wouldn't have served as an excuse for any lie *I* might have told. I don't remember ever asking my mother for an explanation. Perhaps I thought she would explain it with a reason that would once again leave me hanging.

One final example. In those days, when I was six or seven, my sister and I were each given ten pennies every week to put into the collection plate at Sunday school. But, having been cautioned, in a general way, to look out for the cost of things in everyday life, the cost as compared to the value, and not to waste money—we were not a wealthy family, and it was, after all, the Depression—I looked over the cost and the value of Sunday school and decided it wasn't worth ten pennies. So week after week I only put five into the collection plate, and kept the other five in my Sunday pocketbook. After a while, my pocketbook got a little heavy, and my mother opened it to see why. She was horrified. Another spanking for me. And another mystification: When does a caution apply? When was I supposed to make up my own mind about the value of something, and when was I supposed to measure by someone else's yardstick? But I don't think I ever asked about this. I seem only to have stored it away to wonder about. I am still wondering.

These are only four examples, but they'll do. I spent the next few years growing up without changing much, still observing irrationalities, still always asking "Why?" and still getting not much in the form of an answer. But at the same time I too was becoming irrational. Married, finally, and a mother myself, I too lied to my children about Santa Claus. I too said things like "Whose pears are these in the sink?" which often took a form just as familiar: You look at your child, who is scribbling on the wall, and you say, "What are you doing?"

To top it all off, when my children asked *why*, about this situation or that, I seem to have chosen to answer, "Because that's the way things are." This isn't much better than saying, "Because

I said so," but it's a little better. It tells more of the truth. It just stops too soon. If said correctly, it would be: "That's the way things are, because all of us grown-ups are mad, and you are in training."

I grew up, as most of us do, surrounded by a lot of rules. They were all pretty basic, regulating behavior in private as well as public. Rules weren't *laws*, exactly. The *government* wasn't telling you not to kick your sister. But as soon as you were old enough to draw the *attention* of the government, it told you plenty. I observed all these rules and laws to the letter, because I didn't like to lose the approval of my mother *or* the police department. I didn't want to get spanked *or* go to jail. I became, at last, what you see before you: the kind of grown-up who always stops at stop signs, and who never goes through the ten-item line at the grocery with more than ten items. I had learned to accept the premise that it isn't up to me, an average citizen, to obey only the *convenient* laws put forward by the government. Laws are there to be obeyed, whether they're convenient or not. If the government finds out that you've thrown your pears in the sink, you're going to have to answer for it. A great many people throw their pears in the sink anyway, believing that the government won't ever find out, and most of the time they're right. In Providence, where I live now, someone has pointed out that red lights and stop signs aren't laws at all to Rhode Islanders, but only suggestions. You have to wonder how things hold together. Somehow they do hold together. It's just that there's no rational reason for it.

Long before Rhode Island, though, as I was growing up in

Ohio, I was becoming aware that parents and governments can make as many rules and laws as they want to, but none of it will make a particle of difference to the natural world.

Moving from southwestern Ohio up to a suburb of Cleveland on the shores of Lake Erie was the event that began my education in this aspect. I was eleven years old. People who've never lived near the Great Lakes have never seen what is known in weather circles as "the lake effect." Great Lakes storms in all seasons are dramatic, violent, and beautiful. They also come along whenever they feel like it, and don't give the least kind of a damn about humanity. All parts of nature are pretty much like that. Remember the lyrics to "Ol' Man River," which ask, and please forgive my paraphrasing: What does the Mississippi care if the world's got troubles?

So here, on the one hand, were the lessons I was getting about how human beings, especially mothers, Sunday school teachers, and policemen, are in control of just about everything, and yet there, on the other hand, were lessons showing that human beings, whatever their professions, were in control of almost nothing. There was and is no rational way to put these two things together. Nevertheless, put them together we must.

And of course, World War II was getting under way for America along about then. Europe was a complete mess, and Asia wasn't much good, either. So here we were praising the Lord and passing the ammunition, as the popular song had it, and starting out to save the world, which meant having to end the world for huge numbers of Europeans and Asians, soldiers and civilians both. There's no other way to fight a war. We did what we had to do. But none of it sat very well with what I heard in church. I was in real church by that time, not Sunday school, and I was observing that religion lives uneasily with war, in spite of what we'd been taught about the Crusades, and in spite of hymns like "Onward, Christian Soldiers." A great deal of irrational reasoning is required. And yet, and yet, the sun came up every morning, and lake-effect storms swept across northern Ohio in every season, just the same as always. Everything was utterly different, and everything was exactly the same, and there's nothing rational about that.

What it all seems to come down to is that we humans have a very slim grip on the definition of what's rational. The societies we have created, here and everywhere else around the world, are messy, unjust, and dangerous. But each society believes those adjectives are descriptive only of all the *other* societies, while it *itself* is fair, tidy, and safe. We'd get along with each other a lot better if we could admit that we are all pretty much alike regardless of what society we belong to, but that seems to go against the grain.

Well, but when you remember how young this planet is, compared to much of the universe, what else can we expect of ourselves? A while ago, someone said that if you laid out the age of the Earth as a vertical as tall as the Empire State Building, you could place a thin dime on the very topmost part and that would be the total age of humanity. We haven't been around very long. A moment ago we were cavemen, and a moment before that we were apes. At least, if you believe in evolution, that's what we were. So if we've still got a lot of ape in us, where's the surprise? We are deeply and anxiously self-congratulatory and egotistical, but maybe we have to be in order to believe we're in control. We do, after all, have to believe we're in control, and that means inventing all sorts of reasonable reasons for our irrational behavior, which we spell out for each other gravely every chance we get. There is a lot of gravity during an election year, isn't there? A great deal of *reasoning*—just as there is in *Alice in Wonderland.* Do you remember the story told by the Dormouse at the mad tea party? Allow me, with a few cuts here and there, to refresh your memories, first reminding you, in case you've forgotten, that *treacle*, referred to here, is a blend of molasses, sugar, and corn syrup:

"Once upon a time there were three little sisters," the Dormouse began . . . ; "and their names were Elsie, Lacie, and Tillie; and they lived at the bottom of a well—"

"What did they live on?" said Alice, who always took a great interest in questions of eating and drinking.

"They lived on treacle," said the Dormouse, after thinking a minute or two.

"They couldn't have done that, you know," Alice gently remarked; "they'd have been ill."

*"So they were," said the Dormouse; "*very ill.*"*

Alice tried to fancy to herself what such an extraordinary way of living would be like, but it puzzled her too much: so she went on: "But why did they live at the bottom of a well?" . . .

> *The Dormouse again took a minute or two to think about it, and then said, "It was a treacle-well . . . And so these three little sisters—they were learning to draw, you know—"*
>
> *"What did they draw?" said Alice . . .*
>
> *"Treacle," said the Dormouse, without considering at all, this time . . .*
>
> *"But I don't understand," [said Alice.] "Where did they draw the treacle from?"*
>
> *"You can draw water out of a water-well," said the Hatter; "so I should think you could draw treacle out of a treacle-well—eh, stupid?"*
>
> *"But they were in the well," Alice said to the Dormouse, not choosing to notice this last remark.*
>
> *"Of course they were," said the Dormouse; "—well in."*

And the charm of all this is that the Dormouse, the Mad Hatter, and the March Hare are serenely, and all the way *irrationally,* reasonable. It reminds me very much of a televised congressional investigation.

If you grow up puzzling about irrationality, and then if you begin writing stories, all these puzzling things are bound to turn up in what you write. I wanted to be a children's book illustrator, and that meant, obviously, that I would need children's stories to illustrate. I hadn't ever thought about being a writer. But I discovered right away, when I began trying to write, that many puzzling and difficult moral and ethical questions insisted on cropping up, as they do in many stories for children. At least they do in some kinds of stories, and those seem to be the kinds of stories *I* tell. After all, if you have any memory at all about your concerns when you were very small, you will know that this is when such questions first arise. I seem to have a particularly vivid memory of those years. In some ways, they were more interesting to me than many of the years that have come along since. Still, the questions themselves are scarcely unique to *me*. They are questions we all have in common. Some of us don't give them a lot of head room, and that's all right, but for those of us who do, stories can be useful. Well—useful up to a point. My stories don't offer answers, because I don't know the answers. Maybe there aren't any. All I'm trying to do is present the questions.

We began, centuries ago, telling stories in an attempt to explain humanity's basic mysteries. And then science started to redraw our conception of things like the universe, health, death, and other natural phenomena. Take water, for instance. For hundreds of years, we believed it had magical qualities. I think this is because we knew it gave and maintained life. But now we know there is nothing magical about it. We learned from a British scientist named Henry Cavendish in the late 1700s that water is only a combination of oxygen and hydrogen. And as for this planet Earth, it may be vital to the only kind of life we know, but at the same time it is nothing more than a meaningless speck in the endlessness of space.

Well, we know these things, but knowing them isn't much help. The knowledge is simply not enough. Too many questions still remain. How can something be vital, and at the same time be meaningless? The word *endlessness*, itself, as a description of a dimension, is inconceivable, and therefore completely unsatisfying.

My sister said once that trying to understand space brought her to the outermost extent of her intelligence. She came to a place, she told me, where she didn't even know what it was that she wasn't understanding. We all know that feeling. And even right here on our own planet, it is impossible to watch the raging water in our Great Lakes in the middle of a storm and hold on to our self-importance by telling ourselves it's only hydrogen and oxygen flinging themselves around out there. So—we go right on telling stories. We need to. It may be irrational, but at the same time it's perfectly reasonable.

Most of the stories I've told fall into this category—the category of stories that deal with the questions left over after we're told that all the questions have been answered. This kind of story isn't everybody's cup of tea. I know that perfectly well, and even if I didn't, children often remind me. A letter I got last year from some boys in Boston told me that *Tuck Everlasting* would have been a lot better if it had had some dirt-bike racing in it. Maybe so, but I have to write the kind of story I write, because it's the only kind of story that, for *me*, anyway, is worth the immense difficulty of writing.

And into these stories of mine go all the questions about what's right at any given moment—all the questions like the one about the ten Sunday school pennies. Years ago, not long after *Tuck Everlasting* was published, I was on a gig somewhere and was approached afterward by a young librarian who was genuinely disturbed by the fact that I had let Mae Tuck kill the man in the yellow suit. We talked about it briefly. I asked her what she would have done if she'd known ahead of time what World War II was going to do to the world. Would she have killed Adolf Hitler before it all began, if she'd had the opportunity? She was horrified by this question, and turned away without answering. Well, of course she was horrified. It's not a pretty thought. But it's a very important question. At least, I think so. And of course, where *Tuck Everlasting* is concerned, there's more than philosophy involved in the killing. I don't like violence in any form, but I got right up to the point when the man in the yellow suit was dragging Winnie Foster away, and I knew what I would have done if I'd been Mae Tuck. I knew that if someone had broken into *my* house and had tried to drag one of *my* children away, I'd have grabbed anything that came to hand and bashed him as hard as I could. I wouldn't have paused to think it over. And neither would any other female, two legs or four, in all of the natural world. This is the simple truth. And when you write for children, the truth is vital.

Violence goes against every rule and law in the land. Yes. But there are times when it's justified. Well, aren't there? Aren't there times when we have to act as the occasion demands? Isn't that what a war of defense is mostly about? I don't know for sure. All I know is that it's adults who are troubled by that scene in *Tuck Everlasting*. I get a lot of letters from children about the story, and if they mention that scene at all, they tell me that they didn't like it, but they know Mae did what she had to do, and they are satisfied. They invariably say that the man in the yellow suit got what he deserved. This is not because children have been warped by television or any other outside influence. This is because we are all somehow born with a strong sense of justice. Why else say so often, "It's not fair!" Why else wonder why Mildred got to steal my sister's doll underwear while I got a bloody nose for borrowing her new scooter? We laugh at such things remembered from our early lives, and we laugh at them in the lives of our own children. But finally, at bottom, they aren't really funny. They are our earliest attempts to find and examine *reasons*, irrational or not. Is it all right to go against the rules when you're growing up? No. Rules are there for guidance and protection. Except sometimes. Is it all right to kill people? No. Killing is immoral and illegal. Except sometimes. And so, while we're learning the rules as we grow up, we're observing at the same time the contradictions, the exceptions, the irrationalities. There's no way to protect children from all that, and a good thing, too, because they're going to need the truth.

What a puzzle it all turns out to be! We would do better with it if we didn't have so frantic a need to prove ourselves quick and powerful and in control, to prove to ourselves and others that we *matter*. It's hard, though, because we *do* matter to ourselves. It's just that we don't matter to thunderstorms and oceans and time and the endlessness of space. I think, finally, that we are all mad because of being pulled in half between these two plain truths.

There are three ways to deal with it, I think. You can put time and space out of your head, and live only in and with the tangible world. Or—you can ignore the tangible world and go live on a mountaintop where you can contemplate time and space. Or—you can say to yourself that it's impossible to make sense of it all, so we might as well throw up our hands and have as good a time as we can manage in the time we've got.

I don't know when I decided to adopt the third alternative, but I think I know why. Certainly my father had a lot to do with it because, once you got past politics, he knew how to see irrationalities and the ways in which they affect us, and he knew how to laugh at them. My mother was good at laughing, too, but the simple fact is that the marriage between her and my father was a first-class example of living with two plain and opposing truths. My father was a very conservative Republican, and my mother was a very liberal Democrat, and at the end of every election day, he would say to her, "I suppose you canceled my vote again," and she would reply, "I certainly did." But they loved each other anyway, and had what I truly believe was a very happy life together.

So—well—I think I grew up questioning the contradictions, as we all do, but finally admiring the way we human beings always manage, however clumsily, to build a footing out of not much, and then dance on it. Because we do dance on it, here and everywhere else in the world, regardless of science, religion, and politics. And we dance pretty well, thank you very much. It's mad to dance on such a footing, because collapse is always imminent, but we do it anyway. There's a lot to be learned from that. Somehow, in spite of everything, we manage to build. We have always managed to build, even right after we've managed to destroy.

What does this have to do with children and their books? Maybe not much, except that the fact is, children learn early to laugh *and* to reason, to recognize irrationalities for what they are but at the same time work out reasonable ways to deal with this vital but meaningless speck of a planet they've inherited. Writers write the stories that ease their own uncertainties, of course, and that makes most of our work pretty subjective. But for people like me whose childhoods are so real and so ever-present, I think that for the most part what we have to say are things our readers have no trouble understanding.

And I've come to recognize one other thing: I believe I had a perfect right to throw my pears in the sink, that day so long ago. Not as a way of breaking the rules, but as a way of expressing my own views and preferences. I believe we all have that right *today, now,* whatever age we may be. As long as we're willing to pay the consequences. We have the right to follow our own sense of what matters. I mean, I had the right not to put dirt-bike racing into *Tuck Everlasting.* I wrote back to the boys who thought it would have been a good idea, and I told them that if *they'd* written the story, they could have put anything they wanted into it. But, I told them, by the time they wrote to me, it was way too late for changes. The book was already twenty-five years old, and rather set in its ways. But it has occurred to me since that maybe they'll all get jobs with the Disney Studios when they grow up. At Disney, it's never too late for change. It's never too irrational, either. But, well, so what? Remember the scene in *Alice in Wonderland* where Alice comes across the Cheshire cat sitting in a tree? She asks him:

"Would you tell me, please, which way I ought to go from here?"

"That depends a good deal on where you want to get to," said the Cat.

"I don't much care where—" said Alice.

"Then it doesn't matter which way you go," said the Cat.

"—so long as I get somewhere," *Alice added as an explanation.*

"Oh, you're sure to do that," said the Cat, "if you only walk long enough."

Alice felt that this could not be denied, so she tried another question. "What sort of people live about here?"

"In that *direction," the Cat said, waving its right paw round, "lives a Hatter: and in* that *direction," waving the other paw, "lives a March Hare. Visit either you like: they're both mad."*

"But I don't want to go among mad people," Alice remarked.

"Oh, you can't help that," said the Cat: "we're all mad here."

Amen to that, my dears. We may be irrational, but we can be reasonable, too, and we can laugh. If we've forgotten about that somewhere along the way, children can remind us. Children can show us how.

Notes

Happy Endings? Of Course, and Also Joy

First published in the *New York Times Book Review*, November 8, 1970.

7 "There is no such thing": P. L. Travers, "A Kind of Visitation" (a review of *The Animal Family* by Randall Jarrell), *New York Times Book Review*, November 21, 1965.

10 "muddy streams of conciousness": Isaac Bashevis Singer, "I See the Child as a Last Refuge," *Signposts to Criticism of Children's Literature.* Ed. R. Bator (Chicago: American Library Association, 1983), 50–54.

The Child as Chimpanzee

First published under the title "How Can We Write Children's Books If We Don't Know Anything About Children?" in *Publishers Weekly*, vol. 200, no. 3 (July 19, 1971), 64–66.

The Great American Novel for Children—and Why Not?

Presented at the Loughborough International Summer Seminar on Children's Literature, Towson State College, 1973. Reprinted in the *Horn Book Magazine*, vol. 50, no. 2 (March/April 1974), 176–185.

31 "What makes [works of literature] great": Van Wyck Brooks, *The Writer in America* (New York: Dutton, 1953), 20, 26–27.

35 "popular success": Brooks, *Writer in America*, 161.

37 "Life begins with a cry": Arnold Gesell and Frances L. Ilg, *The Child from Five to Ten* (New York: Harper, 1946), 276, 301.

38 "Good stories": Gesell and Ilg, *Child from Five*, 302.

42 "Art that merely soothes": Anthony Burgess, "For Permissiveness, with Misgivings," *New York Times Magazine*, July 1, 1973, 19–20.

You Must Go Home Again

The Miriam A. Wessel Lecture, Detroit Public Library, April 1978. Reprinted under the title "The Fantastic Voyage" in the *Five Owls*, vol. 1, no. 6 (July/August 1987).

50 "What we want": Russell P. MacFall, *To Please A Child: A Biography of L. Frank Baum, Royal Historian of Oz* (Chicago: Reilly & Lee, 1961), 131.

54 "the forgotten language": Carl Sagan, *The Dragons of Eden: Speculations on the Evolution of Human Intelligence* (New York: Random House, 1977), 180.

58 "Myths are things": Sagan, *Dragons of Eden*, 7.

Saying What You Think

Presented at the Library of Congress, November 16, 1981, for National Children's Book Week. Reprinted in the *Quarterly Journal of the Library of Congress*, vol. 39, no. 2 (Spring 1982), 80–89.

The Way We Were—and Weren't

Presented at the Everychild Conference, 1985. Reprinted, in edited form, under the title "Who is 'The Child'?" in the *Horn Book Magazine*, vol. 62, no. 2 (March/April 1986), 161–166.

Something Has to Happen

First published in the *Lion and the Unicorn*, vol. 9 (1985), 7–10.

The Roots—and Branches—of Fantasy

First published under the title "The Roots of Fantasy" in the *Children's Literature Assembly Bulletin*, vol. 12, no. 2 (Spring 1986), 2–4.

Easy Does It

Presented at the Missouri Library Association Conference, 1986. Reprinted in *Top of the News*, American Library Association, vol. 43 (Summer 1987).

Metamorphosis

Presented at Simmons College, 1987. Reprinted, in edited form, in the *Horn Book Magazine*, vol. 64, no. 5 (September/October 1988), 582–589.

A Question from Justine

Keynote address, Annual Reading and Writing Conference for Teachers, University of North Carolina at Charlotte, 1987. Reprinted as "The Mad Tea Party Maxim: Or How Books Don't Always Mean What the Writer Intended" in *Children's Literature in Education*, vol. 22, no. 2 (1991), 89–96.

144 "Children's literature is a complicated": Hamida Bosmajian, "*Charlie and the Chocolate Factory* and Other Excremental Visions," *Lion and the Unicorn*, vol. 9 (1985), 36.

147 "the universal subconscious fear": Michael Tunnell, "Books in the Classroom," *Horn Book Magazine*, vol. 63, no. 4 (July/August 1987), 509.

The Purpose of Literature—and Who Cares?

Anne Carroll Moore Lecture, The New York Public Library, 1989. Reprinted in *School Library Journal*, vol. 36, no. 3 (March 1990), 150–152.

154 "because there are no easy solutions": Mark Jonathan Harris, "It's So Much Easier to Write about the Rich," *New York Times Book Review*, November 12, 1989.

Darkness and Light

Not previously published.

Protecting Children's Literature

Presented at Simmons College, 1990. Reprinted in the *Horn Book Magazine*, vol. 66, no. 6 (November/December 1990), 696–703.

Beacons of Light
Presented at Simmons College, 1993.

Finding Paths
Presented at Children's Literature New England, Radcliffe College, 1999.

New World, No World
Presented at Simmons College, 2001.

220 "If you say something negative": Robin Finn, "Filmmakers Tremble, and Gladiators Fall Apart," *New York Times Book Review*, May 16, 2001.

221 "I stopped fretting": Roger Sutton, "Bring Out Your Dead," *Horn Book Magazine*, vol. 77, no. 4 (July/August 2001), 387–388.

226 "Earth should remain": Michael D. Lemonick, "The End," *Time*, vol. 157, no. 25 (June 25, 2001), 48.

We're All Mad Here
Zena Sutherland Lecture, Chicago Public Library, 2004. Reprinted in the *Horn Book Magazine*, vol. 80, no. 5 (September/October 2004), 507–518.